INFORMATION TECHNOLOGY (IT) PROFESSIONALS

PRACTICAL CAREER GUIDES

Series Editor: Kezia Endsley

Culinary Arts, by Tracy Brown
Dental Assistants and Hygienists, by Kezia Endsley
Education Professionals, by Kezia Endsley
Fine Artists, by Marcia Santore
First Responders, by Kezia Endsley
Health and Fitness Professionals, by Kezia Endsley
Information Technology (IT) Professionals, by Erik Dafforn
Medical Office Professionals, by Marcia Santore
Skilled Trade Professionals, by Corbin Collins

INFORMATION TECHNOLOGY (IT) PROFESSIONALS

A Practical Career Guide

ERIK DAFFORN

ROWMAN & LITTLEFIELD
Lanham • Boulder • New York • London

Published by Rowman & Littlefield
An imprint of The Rowman & Littlefield Publishing Group, Inc.
4501 Forbes Boulevard, Suite 200, Lanham, Maryland 20706
www.rowman.com

6 Tinworth Street, London SE11 5AL, United Kingdom

British Library Cataloguing in Publication Information Available

Library of Congress Cataloging-in-Publication Data

Names: Dafforn, Erik, author.
Title: Information technology (IT) professionals : a practical career guide
  / Erik Dafforn.
Description: Lanham : Rowman & Littlefield, [2020] | Series: Practical
  career guides | Includes bibliographical references. | Summary: "IT
  Professionals includes interviews with professionals in the field,
  covers three main areas of this field that have proven to be stable,
  lucrative, and growing professions. · Programmers · Web Developers · IT
  Specialists"—Provided by publisher.
Identifiers: LCCN 2019039251 (print) | LCCN 2019039252 (ebook) | ISBN
  9781538111772 (paperback) | ISBN 9781538111789 (epub)
Subjects: LCSH: Information technology—Vocational guidance.
Classification: LCC T58.5 .D34 2020 (print) | LCC T58.5 (ebook) | DDC
  004.023—dc23
LC record available at https://lccn.loc.gov/2019039251
LC ebook record available at https://lccn.loc.gov/2019039252

Contents

Introduction

Welcome to Information Technology

*T*hink about the following businesses or careers and try to figure out what they all have in common:

- A hospital
- An advertising agency
- A bakery
- A large department store
- A musician

Each of these businesses or careers uses employees or outside services to perform its tasks. And each one provides a good or a service to the public.

Because you're reading a book about information technology (IT), you probably know the answer. Each of these organizations, in one way or another, uses information technology in a way that helps it perform better, deliver its product with more efficiency and safety, and understand its customers' needs with more precision.

- A hospital must make sure that it keeps flawless records about patient care, such as what patients need and when they need it. And patient data must be kept safe from intruders but still be instantly accessible to doctors and other healthcare workers so they can make split-second decisions for the patient's health.
- An advertising agency makes recommendations to its clients about what sort of advertising makes sense based on the clients' potential customers. Does a particular client need a new website? Does it make sense to advertise at bus stops and on billboards, or would it be better to buy some ad time on television?
- A bakery needs to know exactly how much of each ingredient to buy because it has limited storage space. It also needs to track how popular

its new pies are, so it can decide whether to keep baking them or try something different.

- A large department store has thousands of products for sale. It needs to have a good understanding of whether some products sell better in the store or on its website, and it also needs to listen to social media to know how people are talking about the store and its products. This helps it make purchasing decisions for the next season.
- A musician just starting out needs to record his or her music in a way that makes it easy to share with fans, and also needs to let those fans know where he or she will be performing in the near future.

While these businesses are different in many ways, they are similar because each one needs IT to help it succeed. Information technology is a broad category of products and services that includes hardware (specific computer and networking parts), software (programs and applications that tell the hardware how to act), and skills that tie hardware and software together, with the end goal of helping users get the solutions they need to meet their goals.

As described in the preceding list, a solution may be a safe, hack-proof storage system for patients' medical data or it may be information collected about which cupcakes sell the best on Saturdays. Information technology is the industry that designs, tests, implements, and maintains the types of systems described in this list.

> "Information technology and business are becoming inextricably interwoven. I don't think anybody can talk meaningfully about one without talking about the other."
> —Bill Gates, cofounder of Microsoft

At its core, information technology can be described very simply as just pieces of data and the methods and tools that people use to store and use that data.

A Career in Information Technology

A career in IT is almost impossible to describe in just a few sentences, because it can encompass such a wide variety of roles, responsibilities, and locations. Here are just a few characteristics of a career in IT:

- You will work with many different kinds of people—people of all ages, experience levels, and roles within the company.
- Often you will work on a team with other IT professionals whose skills and talents complement each other. Occasionally, however, you might work on projects by yourself.
- Sometimes your customers—that is, the people for whom you perform tasks and complete projects—will be people or companies that buy things from your company. Other times, your customers will be people who work for the same company that you do.
- Even though you might be out of college by the time you get your first job, your education will never be finished. IT professionals typically keep educating themselves on the latest technologies all throughout their careers.

A career in IT will expose you to a fast-paced environment that requires problem solving, exposure to all different kinds of people, and a never-ending education.

Because information technology is such a broad career path, there are many different ways to divide it into categories. For simplicity, this book breaks IT into six main areas:

- Technical support staff
- Programmers
- Web developers
- Systems analysts
- Network engineers
- Security analysts

What are jobs in these areas like? Are jobs in one category only, or is there some overlap? What education, skills, and certifications do you need to succeed in these fields? What are the salary and job outlook for each category? And what are the pros and cons of each type of IT job? This book answers these questions, and many more, in the following chapters.

The IT Market Today

The IT market in the United States is in excellent shape, and it will probably remain one of the most stable, productive forces in the US job market for years to come. The US Bureau of Labor Statistics expects that between now and 2026, the IT job market will grow 13 percent, which is greater growth than average. Information technology careers also have a median salary that is more than twice as high as the average income for all jobs.

The Bureau of Labor Statistics website (https://www.bls.gov/) has current information about the IT professions discussed in this book, as well as related professions. You can find specific information about each of the areas described in this book at the following websites:

- *Technical support staff:* https://www.bls.gov/ooh/computer-and-infor mation-technology/computer-support-specialists.htm
- *Programmers:* https://www.bls.gov/ooh/computer-and-information -technology/computer-programmers.htm
- *Web developers:* https://www.bls.gov/ooh/computer-and-information -technology/web-developers.htm

- *Systems analysts:* https://www.bls.gov/ooh/computer-and-information -technology/computer-systems-analysts.htm
- *Network engineers:* https://www.bls.gov/ooh/computer-and-information -technology/network-and-computer-systems-administrators.htm
- *Security analysts:* https://www.bls.gov/ooh/computer-and-information -technology/information-security-analysts.htm

Every industry has threats, however, and the US IT labor market is no different. Competition from countries overseas is fierce and will continue to challenge the best talent in the United States. This is one reason most IT managers insist that continuing education is a smart move for information technology workers.

What Does This Book Cover?

This book takes you through the steps to see if a career in IT might be right for you. It also gives you practical advice on how to pursue an education that will set you up to be a successful candidate for the type of IT job you might want. Here's what each chapter of the book covers:

- Chapter 1 describes the many specific paths that an IT career can take. From hardware to software, back end to front end, this chapter gives you an idea of the many different types of IT career options that exist.
- Chapter 2 describes the education requirements that you should know as you think about entering the IT field. It talks about steps that you can take as early as high school to prepare yourself, and it also describes the things you can do outside of class to help yourself be ready for an IT education.
- Chapter 3 looks at educational options that will lead you to a job in IT. It discusses academic requirements, costs, and financial aid options that will help you understand your economic options, and it will list the top college programs for an IT education.
- Chapter 4 helps you develop the tools that will help you prepare to interview for jobs and internships. It also helps with cover letters, explains how to dress for meetings, and helps you understand what employers expect out of people looking for jobs.

Throughout each chapter, you'll read interviews with real people, at various stages of their careers, who chose IT as a career path. They offer real advice, encouragement, and ways to know if IT is something that might be right for you.

Where Do You Start?

Take a deep breath and jump right into chapter 1, which will answer lots of questions you might already have, including questions about job availability, salary, and whether your personality is built for a career in IT. If you already know that IT is the career path you want, it's still a good idea to read chapter 1, because it offers insight into specific pros and cons of IT that you might not have considered.

Chapter 1 also features an interview with Michael Mattax, a man who has worked in many different IT roles so far in his fast-moving career. He shares some valuable information about what it's like to work in a start-up company,

Your future awaits!

how his education shaped his career path, and the characteristics that make strong IT professionals.

Summary

Now that you've read the introduction, you might have an idea of whether information technology is for you. It described a lot of different businesses that each use IT in their own unique ways. It discussed how the book's chapters are laid out, and it explained a little bit about what's coming up in the next chapter.

Even if you're not sure about information technology, keep reading, because chapter 1 is going to give you some really good information about the industry. It will break down the many different types of careers within IT, and will be helpful in determining which area of IT you might find most interesting.

Why Choose a Career in Information Technology?

*I*n the introduction, you learned that the information technology field is growing and is expected to be a strong career path for a long time. At the same time, you learned that it's a competitive industry and that to succeed in it, you'll need to keep learning new techniques, languages, and technologies all throughout your career.

This book is not designed to convince you that you should pursue an IT career. Instead, its goal is to thoroughly describe various careers within IT to help you decide whether it's something you'd like to explore. IT is an interesting career choice because IT professionals work in every type of industry and business imaginable—from architecture to zoos, from the largest companies in the world to the smallest nonprofits.

This chapter discusses six key fields in IT, covering the basic duties and tasks involved with each. After reading this chapter, you will have a good understanding of six different types of IT jobs, and you will start to determine if one of them is a good fit for you. Let's start with discussing what IT professionals do.

What Do Information Technology Workers Do?

If you have used a phone, watched a video, used a computer, printed a paper, or ordered something online, you are probably aware of some of the ways information technology has made it easier for you to do things you want to do. IT workers program phone apps, create video-editing software, ensure that networks are transferring data properly, and make sure you can track your package after ordering. In short, IT workers consistently build, maintain, and fix the products, services, and systems that we use every day.

Information technology also exists in places you might not expect. Even buying dog food or playing soccer at the park involves IT behind the scenes in more ways than you can probably imagine. IT has become so integrated into our lives that it's hard to count how many ways it affects us. That's one of the reasons the information technology industry offers so many different opportunities and different types of jobs.

For now, however, it's important to understand the six main types of IT careers this book covers:

- Technical support staff
- Programmers
- Web developers
- Systems analysts
- Network architects
- Security analysts

The following sections discuss each one of these fields in depth, including the basic tasks and duties involved in the job, the level of education typically required, and the job outlook for that specific field over the next several years.

Technical Support Staff

Technical support staff (also sometimes called computer support, tech support, IT support, and other similar terms) offer guidance, advice, and help to organizations and to specific users. Because information technology takes so many different forms, technical support staff provide this assistance at many different levels:

- *Hardware:* A hardware support specialist helps users diagnose, repair, or replace specific pieces of hardware, including monitors, printers, keyboards, or specific components of a computer, such as network adapters (the specific products that help computers talk to other devices). Often these technical support staff are the first people who get a call when a user has a problem. In addition, hardware support helps roll out new equipment to users on a broad scale. For example, if it's time to upgrade

Studying and learning new things is a big part of every IT career.

an entire group of workers to a new computer system, hardware support will help each user set up and become familiar with those new computers.

- *Software:* A software support specialist helps users with specific applications so that the users can be as productive as possible, whether the application is used for work or for personal reasons. For example, a software support specialist might help a user learn a new version of a spreadsheet program to do his or her accounting job better. Similarly, a software support specialist for a phone manufacturer (such as Samsung or Apple) might help new users understand the operating systems of their phones, how to download and use apps, and so on.
- *Network:* A network support specialist typically helps users who need machines or devices to communicate with each other. The list of devices is nearly endless, and it could contain everything from computers and peripherals to tablets, phones, appliances, and medical devices. For example, a worker might need assistance hooking up a computer to a printer, or a company might have problems being able to connect to the internet.

In large companies, all of these types of technical support might be per-formed by different people or teams. In other words, you might be software support staff, and other people might be hardware or network support staff. In some smaller companies, however, workers might be expected to support all types of issues, from hardware to software to network and beyond. When you begin your education, you'll probably have exposure to multiple types of sup-port scenarios. This will help you decide whether you enjoy hardware, software, networking, or some combination of them.

> "There are, by far, more people to work and collaborate with on various projects than I imagined. It has been a terrific additional learning experience."—Amanda Gunnels, development and IT administrator

While most information technology jobs involve some amount of inter-action with other people (users, managers, customers, coworkers, and so on), technical support staff usually spend a very large amount of time with others. As technical support, you will often be among the first people called when there's a problem, and your ability to remain patient while assisting users is important. Beyond the tasks described previously, the typical tasks of a techni-cal support person include:

- Listening to users as they describe the issues they need you to fix
- Asking users questions to help diagnose the exact problem so you can fix it efficiently
- Describing the process users need to follow to fix their problems
- Repairing computers and other devices as needed
- Installing new hardware and software and training users to use it effi-ciently[1]

If you enjoy working with people, love to know how things work, and like a fast-paced environment, a technical support position might be good for you. In some ways, technical support staff are like the doctors of the IT world. Peo-ple come to them with problems, and they diagnose those problems and make recommendations or treat the problem until it's better.

On the other hand, many support staff work long hours, and sometimes they need to be on call overnight or during the weekend. There is a lot of stress, because the success of the company rides on its IT systems. So consider these facts while you learn more.

JOB OUTLOOK

The Bureau of Labor Statistics estimates that between now and 2026, demand for technical support staff will increase by about 11 percent across all different types of support workers. This is slightly lower than the overall growth in computer professions (13 percent) but well above the average growth of all jobs, which is expected to be about 7 percent.

One of the key growth areas in technical support staff is expected to be within the healthcare industry. The healthcare field expects to see large increases in the use of computers, networking, and other technical devices, and the support required to keep those investments running smoothly will grow at a similar rate.

INDUSTRY COMPENSATION

As described earlier in this chapter, there are different types of support specialists. The Bureau of Labor Statistics divides them into computer network support specialists and computer user support specialists. Both types of support specialists earn higher median incomes than most jobs, but network support specialists had a median income of $62,340 in 2017, while computer user support specialists had a median wage of $50,210 in the same year. Both of these salaries are above the median salary for all occupations in 2017, which was $37,690.[2]

EDUCATIONAL REQUIREMENTS

It is not necessarily easy to become a technical support specialist, but becoming a support specialist can be easier than some of the other IT jobs discussed later in this chapter. While many technical support roles, especially within large organizations, require a bachelor's degree, it is possible to get a job with an associate's degree or even with only a few classes after high school.

WHAT IS A MEDIAN INCOME?

Throughout this book, you'll see the term *median income* used frequently. What does it mean? Some people believe it's the same thing as *average income*, but that's not correct. While median income and average income might sometimes be similar, they are calculated in different ways.

The median income is the figure in the middle of the income distribution; half of the workers earn more, and the other half earn less. If this sounds complicated, think of it this way: Suppose there are five support specialists in a company, each with varying skills and experience. Here are their salaries:

- $42,500
- $48,250
- $51,600
- $63,120
- $86,325

What is the median income? In this case, the median income is $51,600, because of the five total positions listed, it is in the middle. Two salaries are higher than $51,600, and two are lower.

The average income is simply the total of all salaries divided by the number of employees. In this case, the average income is $58,359.

Why does this matter? The median income is a more accurate way to measure the various incomes in a set because it's less likely to be influenced by extremely high or low numbers in the total group of salaries. For example, in our example of five incomes, the highest income ($86,325) is much higher than the other incomes, and therefore it makes the average income ($58,359) well higher than most incomes in the group. Therefore, if you base your income expectations on the average, you'll likely be disappointed to eventually learn that most incomes are below it.

But if you look at median income, you'll always know that half the people are above it, and half are below it. That way, depending on your level of experience and training, you'll have a better estimate of where you'll end up on the salary spectrum.

This is not a recommendation against a formal education, of course. Associate's and bachelor's degrees will always increase your odds of getting a job and increase your potential opportunities. However, if college is not an option for you or if you can already show proficiency and knowledge of certain specific support-based concepts and skills without a formal degree, then technical support specialist might be a good option for you.

Programmers

Programmers are in charge of writing code that fulfills specific goals or tasks that are required of a software program. For example, a programmer might write code that takes data from a state-by-state table of sales tax values and applies it to the purchase price of an item in a shopping cart application. Another example would be writing code that gradually dims your phone's screen when the phone's sensor determines that the surrounding light in the room is dim.

While most people associate programming specifically with computers, programmers actually work across many different device types, from transportation (cars and airplanes) to appliances (microwave ovens and refrigerators) to entertainment devices (televisions and home smart speakers).

The tool that each programmer uses is called a programming language. Programming languages use commands, terms, and syntax that enable machines to talk to each other and perform tasks. Different programming languages perform better for different machines and situations. As a result, there are many different programming languages that a person can learn. It's not required to know all of them (there are too many), but most programmers know more than one. Current popular languages include JavaScript, Python, C++, and Ruby.

JOB OUTLOOK

Programmers are one of the few careers in information technology that have a negative job outlook between now and 2026. This means that according to the Bureau of Labor Statistics, fewer programmers will be needed in 2026 than are needed today, with about a 7 percent projected decline in need. If that's the case, you might ask, why is this a recommended job within IT?

There are several reasons why programming is still a potentially wise career choice. First, because IT jobs are so closely related, learning programming languages and serving as a programmer can make it very easy to move to a different job in IT, such as a software developer or network analyst. Second, while fewer programmers may actually be needed, *good* programmers will continue to be needed and valued, even if the overall number needed declines. And third, it's very possible that the way companies describe programmers is changing. Even among programmers and developers themselves, people are more often using the term *developer* to describe what used to be called a programmer.

INDUSTRY COMPENSATION

The median yearly income for computer programmers was $82,240 in 2017. Programmers typically earn different salaries in different industries. For example, programmers working in software companies typically earn more (about $97,000) compared to programmers in manufacturing companies, who earn a median salary of about $82,000. Regardless of these differences, however, the median salary for programmers is right about at the middle of the salary range for IT jobs in general, and well above the median salary of all jobs, which is about $38,000.[3]

EDUCATIONAL REQUIREMENTS

The larger and more formal the organization, the more likely that it will require a bachelor's degree for a programming job. A formal degree program is a great way to learn several different languages, and it will teach you a skill set designed to help you learn further languages down the road.

Even if you have a degree, it will be a good idea to take additional courses, either general programming classes or specific certification courses, throughout your career. This will help you keep your skills sharp, teach you what's new in the market, and ensure that you are aware of the current state of the industry.

LIFE IN A START-UP: ONE JOB, MANY HATS

Michael Mattax (right) with his wife, Shanna. *Courtesy of Michael Mattax.*

Michael Mattax has an interesting job: He works for a company that helps small technical start-ups become real companies. If you want to work for him or with him, get ready: He's the guy who has to get up at 2:00 a.m. to get things moving when things break down, and he'll expect you to know a lot of stuff if you want the job.

He knew in high school that he wanted to be in programming, and his career has confirmed he made the right decision. While he went to college to learn to program, he has encouraging words if you are considering an alternative educational path.

What is your current title and where do you work?

I'm a software engineer at Incipient Labs, a small (three-person) company that builds and launches software start-ups. Previously, I worked for Formstack in many roles: senior software engineer, DevOps, and even product management.

What are your main job duties?

Because I've worked in a start-up environment for most of my career, I've always had to "wear many hats." On a typical day I do technical support, build new features for our products, fix bugs, and help shape our product road map.

Have you had other jobs in IT? What were they?

I've led the engineering team at Formstack, which involved setting product road maps, hiring engineers, and ensuring that our team was delivering new features and fixes that retained and attracted our customers.

I've been in charge of DevOps, which is a bit of a catchall term for someone who manages infrastructure (think networking, servers, availability/performance of a web application) and the tooling that helps software engineers build software.

Did you start your education with the goal of being in IT?

I got into computer programming my last year in high school and knew I wanted to continue with it. I went to college and graduated with a degree in computer science.

What is your formal educational background?

I have a bachelor's degree in computer science.

Did you get all your education at once, or did it occur over time, around jobs?

I did my degree all at once, but with most things you never stop learning, especially in IT, which moves fast. I've learned many programming languages, and almost all of my networking/server infrastructure education has been on the job.

What is a typical day like for you?

I dedicate most of my time in the mornings to customer support and various product meetings. My goal is to be able to program in the afternoons uninterrupted.

What is the most surprising thing about your job?

So many things change in the world of computer programming that not much surprises me. Though one big surprise is that I've seen programmers with degrees from well-known universities struggle in software engineering roles, whereas I've seen self-educated, fresh-out-of-high-school applicants exceed all expectations. The barrier of entry can be low if you have the tech chops and can learn quickly.

What are some things you really like about your job?

I get to make things. Further, I get to make things that other people find helpful (and are willing to pay for!).

Programming is also all about problem solving, tinkering around with solutions, and building (products, features, and so on) from the ground up. There is an art to being able to come up with readable but elegant solutions—being able to "look under the hood" of websites and web applications and see all the "moving parts" is just fascinating to me.

I get to learn new programming languages, tools, technology all the time—it really gives you a sense of accomplishment and a "how far I've come" feeling.

In reality, it's super in demand, it can offer flexibility (such as working from home), and the pay is great.

What are some things you don't like about your job?

Things break, bugs exist. It's often my job to put out fires and wake up at 2:00 a.m. to bring the website back up.

What would be your dream job within the IT field?

Honestly, I love what I'm doing now. Right now, I'd love for one of our software products to take off and become CTO/CEO of it.

What is the possible career trajectory for someone of your position? What would be an ideal job for you to be doing in five to ten years?

There are so many opportunities. It seems like there are two big paths:

- Staying technical: You could be a senior developer, team lead, or in some "architect" role where you're in charge of mentoring developers and designing complex parts of software.
- Management: You might manage products, projects, or teams of developers.

I struggle (and have gone back and forth) between those two paths. Right now I enjoy the technical aspects of my job, but I always see myself going back into management in the future.

What are some characteristics of good IT people? What people really don't fit well in IT?

Top two traits:

- They are good problem solvers. They can take a problem, break it down into smaller ones, and then divide and conquer.
- They know how to learn (pick up on new technology/programming languages, can understand large codebases).

What are some of the challenges facing the IT industry and the people in it?

I think the field is getting more and more competitive. To get in the field, you're going to have to demonstrate that you're the best among the applicants. We give applicants programming challenges to weed out those who don't have the tech chops.

Once you're in the field, it's so hard to stay up to date with the technology that's in demand or new. The best developers find time to experiment or hack on personal projects to learn or understand new technology. The development landscape and tools are mind-blowingly different than they were just three years ago. You always have to be learning.

What advice do you have for young people considering a career in information technology?

My biggest advice is to not depend on a school to teach you what you're going to need in the "real world." If you want to get into IT—start hacking on a personal project, learn new programming languages, build a mobile app, host your own website/blog. Being a tinkerer in the field will show that you can learn, and that you have passion.

_____

Web Developers

Simply put, web developers design, build, and maintain websites. It's an easy job to describe, but the number of tasks involved with website design, construction, and maintenance is immense.

In less than a generation, websites have taken the place of television, radio, and newspapers as the main way people learn about news, businesses, and products. As a result, web developers have a very important job that requires a combination of teamwork, understanding the needs of users, meeting deadlines, measuring success, and knowing what specific technologies should be used to create the best possible website.

There are many ways to divide the tasks that web developers have. Most recently, web developer jobs have been further classified into the following three types of categories:

- *Front-end developers* are generally responsible for the visual part of a website—how it looks, how users interact with it, and how the information is laid out. For example, a front-end developer might be responsible for building new pages on a site, creating the distinct page layout characteristics of a web page (such as the navigation and page layout features), and making sure the site looks good both on a large computer screen and on a smartphone. Front-end developers must have a good understanding of cascading style sheets (CSS), HTML, and scripting languages such as JavaScript.

- *Back-end developers* are more concerned with the underlying structure of a website—what language is used to create it, how fast its pages load within a browser, and any special coding requirements needed for the site to fulfill its duties. For example, a back-end developer might decide to build the site in the Python programming language and choose specific coding methods to store database materials. He or she might also spend time building a scaled coding structure for the site that operates as efficiently with ten thousand web pages as it does with one hundred.
- *Full-stack developers* need to have a strong understanding of the jobs of both the front-end and the back-end developer. They need to have a knowledge of user-interface design, back-end data storage, information retrieval, and integrating additional technology such as ecommerce transactions into a website's list of features. In addition, they often spend time communicating with other teams and managers to learn the goals of the website.

In addition to front-end, back-end, and full-stack developers, you might hear the term *webmaster* in relation to website development, generally referring to someone who is in charge of all aspects of a website, from back-end structural design to front-end interface and everything in between. It can also be used as a term for a person who serves as a point of contact between the organization that owns the website and its users or the general public. Because of the differentiation of web development jobs in recent years, companies now use the term less frequently.

JOB OUTLOOK

The job outlook for web developers appears very strong. The Bureau of Labor Statistics expects that between 2016 and 2026, web development jobs will increase by about 15 percent. This is greater than the overall computer occupation growth expectation of 11 percent, and it's more than twice as strong as the prediction for overall job growth, which is around 7 percent.[4]

The growth for careers in this category is not surprising. Companies are putting more and more resources into their websites while other forms of public relations are leveling off or even declining. With an increase in smartphone usage and ever-increasing download speeds, website development shows no signs of slowing down its pace of rapid development and innovation.

INDUSTRY COMPENSATION

For web developers, the median yearly income was $69,430 in 2018. Just about every type of company has at least one website, and developers for sites in different industries often earn different salaries. For example, developers in noninternet publishing industries have a median wage over $75,360, while developers for advertising and public relations–related businesses have a median wage of just over $66,020.[5]

When it comes to salary and growth potential, there are pros and cons to both large and small companies. Large companies are likely to have multiple web projects going at any given time. They are also more likely to have a path for growth within the company, which can lead to career growth and increased salary over time. On the other hand, working on a large team, it can be harder to stand out from the crowd. Smaller companies are likely to have fewer people on the web development team, and thus rely on each one a great deal. On the other hand, the fewer projects there are, the less varied the work might be, and this might result in fewer growth opportunities. Each company is different, however, so if you're interested in web development, be sure to research companies of all sizes.

EDUCATIONAL REQUIREMENTS

Educational requirements for web developers are among the most flexible of all IT specialists. According to the Bureau of Labor Statistics, requirements for a web developer job can be anything from a high school diploma to a four-year degree, but "an associate's degree in web design or related field is the most common requirement."[6]

Larger, more formal organizations typically have requirements at the higher end of the education spectrum. Still, it's not unheard of to land a job based on skills acquired on your own, or possibly as a project-based consultant. This much is certain: Even if you have a four-year degree, the ability to show your web development skills in the form of a portfolio, sites you've worked on, and/or in an interview is important. If you have an associate's degree or a high school diploma, showing previous results becomes even more important.

And as with all IT jobs, don't assume that your education is done once you get your first job. One characteristic of all IT jobs is that continual learning is essential, regardless of what IT career you pursue. To remain competitive in the job market, it is important to keep your skills fresh. You can do this by taking courses online or locally in your spare time to learn new languages or coding techniques, or by pursuing specific industry certifications.

> "I love the people that work in technology. I think they are some of the most interesting people in the world. You find so many really entertaining and interesting facts about them. They come from all different walks of life. Some come from families that are very wealthy, and some come from families that didn't have anything at all."—Cary Chandler, chief operations officer

Systems Analysts

More than many other workers in the IT field, systems analysts are truly the "big picture" people within a company or organization. Systems analysts straddle the fence between the IT segment of a company and the rest of the organization. Systems analysts must have a good view of IT's role within the company, as well as its costs, benefits, and the role it will play in the company's future.

Systems analysts perform many tasks, including:

- Remaining aware of new technologies to decide whether they would benefit the organization or whether existing systems can do the job
- Presenting a cost/benefit analysis of specific proposed systems to the company's management so they can decide whether to implement it
- Deciding which hardware and software should be chosen to fulfill specific needs within the organization
- Testing and troubleshooting systems to ensure that they're working correctly
- Training users on how to use specific systems and creating documentation that explains the systems in detail[7]

Web developers are in charge of creating websites that appeal to different types of users and look good on multiple device types, including large desktop computers, laptops, tablets, and smartphones.

JOB OUTLOOK

The Bureau of Labor Statistics expects that between 2016 and 2026, the need for qualified systems analysts will grow by about 9 percent. This is slightly ahead of the expected growth for all jobs combined, which is about 7 percent.

More than in some other IT fields, companies hiring systems analysts often prefer to hire analysts with background in the company's particular business category. For example, a systems analyst with a background in the automotive industry will probably have a better chance than someone with no automotive background at being hired by an automaker. This is because the role of the systems analyst is to know the ins and outs of the business itself and how the IT systems will affect it. Contrast this with a front-end web developer, for example, who might need to know very little about automobiles to help construct a carmaker's website.

INDUSTRY COMPENSATION

Computer systems analysts had a median annual salary of $88,740 in 2018. This is relatively high among all computer occupations, where the median salary is $86,320, and more than double the median salary for all occupations combined, which is $38,640.[8]

As with many IT occupations, the job of systems analyst pays better in some industries than in others. Systems analysts in the industry of systems design itself tend to be compensated the best, while analysts in large global businesses, finance, and insurance also are compensated at the high end of the spectrum for systems analysts.[9]

Some systems analysts are contractors, which means they don't have permanent employment. Instead, they work on projects for different clients over a period of weeks, months, or even years. Their compensation is often higher than that of analysts who work for specific companies, but consultants have less job security and might lack additional benefits such as company-sponsored health coverage.

EDUCATIONAL REQUIREMENTS

Among the IT careers discussed in this book, systems analyst jobs are among the most likely to require a bachelor's degree. Further, additional training in business, finance, or some other noncomputer area is often helpful and can make you a more appealing candidate for a systems analyst job. Because systems analysts have to blend knowledge of computer and information systems with the business rules and goals of the company, this additional education can make you a better fit for the job than someone who doesn't have that additional training.

In fact, systems analysis is an IT profession in which a liberal arts degree (a four-year degree that covers a wide variety of course in subjects such as science, psychology, history, math, languages, and music) can give a candidate an advantage because it involves a large amount of varied knowledge.[10]

Some systems analysts choose to get a master's degree, such as a master of business administration (MBA). And like most careers in IT, regardless of your initial education level, it's wise to continue pursuing additional education throughout your career.

Network Architects

Simply put, network architects are the people who design networks. This includes determining what hardware and software is ideal for the network based on the network's list of tasks, number of users, and location.

While every organization might have a slightly different description of what its network architects do, generally network architects:

- Create a visual plan or layout for a network.
- Describe and defend the network plan to management.
- Ensure that information security is a part of the network plan.
- Document the hardware and software needs for users to be able to use the network effectively.[11]

Closely related to network architects are network engineers. While some people use the terms interchangeably, it's more accurate to describe a network architect as someone who designs and visualizes the network and a network engineer as someone who builds, implements, and tests the network. However, either a network engineer or a network architect might both design and build the network. It all depends on the organization. For now, don't get too hung up on the differences, and instead focus on the fact that network architects and engineers are in charge of designing, building, and maintaining networks for both large and small groups of users.

JOB OUTLOOK

The job outlook for network architects and engineers is predicted to be steady over the next several years. Its projected growth through 2026 is about 6 percent. This is about the same as the growth of all occupations, which is predicted to be 7 percent. However, the predicted growth of 6 percent is only about half of the 13 percent growth predicted for all IT jobs combined. This lower predicted growth is due to the surge in popularity of cloud computing services, which already provide many of the services that network architects perform.[12]

This is not to suggest that becoming a network architect is a bad idea. In fact, due to their popularity, cloud computing services are currently the location of many network architecture job opportunities.

INDUSTRY COMPENSATION

Network architects are well paid. Their median yearly income was $109,020 in 2018. This is well higher than the $86,320 median for all computer occupations, and it's nearly three times the $38,640 median of all occupations combined. While this segment of the industry is not growing as quickly as others (although it is still definitely growing), network architecture has a significant financial payoff for those who successfully build careers in it.

As with all segments of IT, some industries pay network architects better than others. Network architects on the higher end of the earning scale typically work for telecom companies (whose core service is building and maintaining communications networks), as well as those who work in large, multilocation businesses and in computer systems design companies. Those on the lower end of the network architecture pay scale often work for educational or governmental institutions.

EDUCATIONAL REQUIREMENTS

As with many IT jobs, the ideal candidate for a networking architecture job will have at least a bachelor's degree in computer science, computer engineering, or a related field. In addition, most architects need to be experienced in other IT roles, such as systems administrator, database administrator, or systems analyst, before working their way up to network architect. This, in part, is why their salaries are at the higher end of the IT spectrum.

Security Analysts

Network security. Cyber security. Internet security. These terms are all related and they describe different angles of information security analysts. Simply put, information security is one of the hottest segments of the IT field right now. When you read about large companies and databases being hacked, you know that it was a failure of network security. But for every company whose data is breached in a security incident, thousands of companies keep their data locked up tight, away from prying eyes. This is the job of the security analyst.

Security analysts learn from each new attack, whether it was carried out on their organization or on another company. By knowing the tools the hackers and data thieves use, they can help their own company create better defenses. In addition to watching other companies, security analysts often attempt to break into their own systems in an attempt to find holes in their security systems and patch them before anyone else identifies the vulnerability.

Typical tasks of the security analyst include:

- Monitoring their company's networks for security breaches
- Becoming familiar with firewalls and tools like encryption to keep data private
- Reporting any security breaches or data loss to management
- Attempting to attack their own networks to simulate a hacking attempt
- Writing security documentation, policies, and procedures for the company's users
- Helping the company's employees understand and properly use the security protocols[13]

JOB OUTLOOK

Security analysts are a hot commodity. This means that they're in great demand, and companies are struggling to fill the slots with qualified workers. In short, there are many opportunities for anyone interested in a career as a security analyst.

The need for security analysts is expected to grow up to 28 percent through 2026. This is more than twice the demand growth for computer occupations in general (13 percent) and four times the expected growth of the average occupation (7 percent).

INDUSTRY COMPENSATION

The median yearly income for network security analysts was $98,350 in 2018.[14] This is about 14 percent higher than the typical computer occupation, and it's well above the median salary of the average occupation, which is $38,640. Those earners on the high end typically work for computer systems design

Network security analysts must not only detect data breaches and prevent future ones, but also document where, when, and ideally by whom the breach took place.

services, or in finance and insurance. Other types of industries that employ security analysts include support services and multilocation organizations.

EDUCATIONAL REQUIREMENTS

Like with most jobs in IT, the ideal candidate for a network security analyst will have a bachelor's degree in a field such as computer science, programming, or a related field.[15] A degree in another field, including liberal arts, is acceptable provided the candidate has a job history that proves his or her experience within IT.

Often network security analysts have already spent time in other IT roles, such as systems administrator or even network architect. This additional experience can provide a good perspective about how networks can be used, misused, and exploited by outside forces.

The Pros and Cons of Being in IT

As you've learned in this chapter, the information technology industry is healthy and poised for growth. Salaries in IT are generally higher than in other fields, and the expected growth in most segments of IT is higher than in many other occupations.

The list of pros of being in IT is long, but here are some of the highlights. Consider these benefits as you think about whether IT is a good field for you:

- Good salaries
- Expected growth in the industry over the next decade
- Dynamic, rapidly changing environment
- Interesting people to work with
- Demand in nearly every type of organization

> "As with every field, it's important to be kind, check your ego, question your assumptions, and work hard. Be willing to accept criticism and the idea that you can't know everything. You will make mistakes, so find a way to become comfortable with that and be willing to learn from those failings."—Scott Dafforn, senior full-stack developer

But not everything about IT is favorable. Like most industries, it has its share of downsides:

- Long hours
- Hectic pace
- Increasing competition from other countries
- Constant need to stay current with technologies and languages
- Lack of diversity within IT staff

Regarding diversity, as you'll read in some of this book's interviews, members of the industry seem encouraged that the diversity issue in IT is slowly getting better, and that succeeding in IT is becoming more merit focused. In other words, their hope is that we're headed toward an IT environment in which earning and keeping a good IT career is based on how well you perform—as opposed to your ethnicity, gender, age, or some other aspect that has nothing to do with job performance.

Summary

Most of this chapter was devoted to describing six different types of IT jobs and a little bit about them:

- Technical support staff
- Programmers
- Web developers
- Systems analysts
- Network architects
- Security analysts

The chapter went into detail about each job type, including example jobs within each category, the job outlook for that particular type of career, its educational requirements, and the compensation you can expect in that line of work compared to other types if IT jobs.

One important thing to remember from this chapter is that even though IT is technically considered a single field or industry, there are many diverse types of jobs that are considered IT jobs in nearly every type of business imaginable. So if there is any industry in which your opportunities are nearly limitless, IT is probably it.

Chapter 2 explores how to build a plan for your future. It discusses everything from educational requirements and certifications to internship opportunities within the IT industry. You'll learn about finding summer jobs and making the most of volunteer work as well. While IT jobs are numerous, the industry is quite competitive. Chapter 2 will discuss how you can set yourself apart from the crowd.

2

Forming a Career Plan

Now that you have some idea what information technology is all about—and maybe you even know which branch of IT you are interested in—it's time to formulate a career plan. For you organized folks out there, this can be a helpful and energizing process. If you're not a naturally organized person, or if the idea of looking ahead and building a plan to adulthood scares you, you are not alone. That's what this chapter is for.

After discussing ways to develop a career plan—there is more than one way to do this!—the chapter dives into the various educational requirements. Finally, it looks at how you can gain experience in your community. Yes, experience will look good on your résumé and in some cases it's even required, but even more important, getting out there and working with IT professionals in various settings is the best way to determine if a career in information technology is really something that you will enjoy. When you find a career that you truly enjoy and have a passion for, it will rarely feel like work at all.

If you still aren't sure if a career in IT is right for you, try a self-assessment questionnaire or a career aptitude test. There are many good ones on the web. As an example, the career resource website Monster.com includes its favorite free self-assessment tools at www.monster.com/career-advice/article/best-free-career-assessment-tools. The Princeton Review also has a very good aptitude test geared toward high schoolers at www.princetonreview.com/quiz/career-quiz.

This chapter could just as well have been titled "How to Not End Up Miserable at Work." Because really, what all this is about is achieving happiness. After all, unless you're independently wealthy, you're going to have to work. That's just a given. If you work for eight hours a day, starting at age eighteen and retiring at age sixty-five, you're going to spend around one hundred thousand hours at work. That's about eleven years! Your life will be much, *much* better if you find a way to spend that time doing something you enjoy, that your personality is well suited for, and that you have the skills to become good at. Plenty of people don't get to do this, and you can often see it in their faces as you go about your day interacting with other people who are working. In all likelihood, they did not plan their careers very well and just fell into a random series of jobs that were available.

So, your ultimate goal should be to match your personal interests and goals with your preparation plan for college and career. Practice articulating your plans and goals to others. When you feel comfortable doing this, that means you have a good grasp of your goals and your plan to reach them.

Planning the Plan

You are on a fact-finding mission of sorts. A career fact-finding plan, no matter what the field, should include these main steps:

- Take some time to consider and jot down your interests and personality traits. Are you a people person, or do you get energy from being alone? Are you creative or analytical? Are you outgoing or shy? Are you organized or creative—or a little of both? Take a career counseling questionnaire (found online or in your guidance counselor's office) to find out more. Consider whether your personal likes and preferences meld well with the careers you are considering.
- Find out as much as you can about the day-to-day work of IT specialists at all levels. In what kinds of environments do they work? Who do they work with? How demanding is the job? What are the challenges? Chapter 1 of this book is designed to help you in this regard.
- Find out about educational requirements and schooling expectations. Will you be able to meet any rigorous requirements? This chapter will help you understand the educational paths you should consider.
- Seek out opportunities to volunteer or shadow those doing the job. Use your critical-thinking skills to ask questions and consider whether this is the right environment for you. This chapter discusses ways to find job-shadowing opportunities and other career-related experiences.
- Look into student aid, grants, scholarships, and other ways you can get help to pay for schooling. It's not just about student aid and scholar-

ships, either. Some larger organizations will pay employees to go back to school to get further degrees.

- Build a timetable for taking required exams such as the SAT and ACT, applying to schools, visiting schools, and making your decision. You should write down all important deadlines and have them at the ready when you need them.

- Continue to look for employment that matters during your college years—internships and work experiences that help you get hands-on experience and knowledge about your intended career.

- Find a mentor who is currently working in your field of interest. This person can be a great source of information, education, and connections. Don't expect a job (at least not at first); just build a relationship with someone who wants to pass along his or her wisdom and experience. Coffee meetings or even e-mails are a great way to start.

The whole point of career planning is not to overwhelm you with a seemingly huge endeavor; it's to maximize happiness.

A mentor can help you in many ways.

YOUR PASSIONS, ABILITIES, AND INTERESTS: IN JOB FORM!

Think about how you've done at school and how things have worked out at any temporary or part-time jobs you've had so far. In your opinion, what are you really good at? What have other people told you you're good at? What are you not very good at right now but would like to become better at? What are you not very good at, and you're okay with not getting better at?

Now forget about work for a minute. In fact, forget about needing to ever have a job again. You've won the lottery—congratulations! Now answer these questions: What are your favorite three ways to spend your time? For each one of those things, can you describe why you think you are particularly attracted to it? If you could get up tomorrow and do anything you wanted all day long, what would it be? These questions can be fun to consider, but they can also lead you to your true passions. The next step is to find the job that sparks your passions.

Where to Go for Help

If you aren't sure where to start, your local library, school library, and guidance counselor's office are great places to begin. Search your local or school library for resources about finding a career path and finding the right schooling that fits your needs and budget. Make an appointment with or e-mail a counselor and ask about taking career interest questionnaires. With a little prodding, you'll be directed to lots of good information online and elsewhere. You can start your research with these sites:

- The Bureau of Labor Statistics' Career Outlook site at www.bls.gov/careeroutlook/home.htm. The US Department of Labor's Bureau of Labor Statistics site doesn't just track job statistics, as you learned in chapter 1. An entire section of the BLS website is dedicated to helping young adults looking to uncover their interests and to match those interests with jobs currently in the market. Check out the section called "Career Planning for High Schoolers." Information is updated based on career trends and jobs in demand, so you'll get timely, practical information as well.

- The Mapping Your Future site at www.mappingyourfuture.org. This site helps you determine a career path and then helps you map out a plan to reach those goals. It includes tips on preparing for college, paying for college, job hunting, résumé writing, and more.
- The Education Planner site at www.educationplanner.org. With separate sections for students, parents, and counselors, this site breaks down the task of planning your career goals into simple, easy-to-understand steps. You can find personality assessments, get tips on preparing for school, read Q&As from counselors, download and use a planner worksheet, read about how to finance your education, and more.
- The TeenLife site at www.teenlife.com. Calling itself "the leading source for college preparation," this site includes lots of information about summer programs, gap year programs, community service, and more. Promoting the belief that spending time out "in the world" outside of the classroom can help students do better in school, find a better fit in terms of career, and even interview better with colleges, this site contains lots of links to volunteer and summer programs.

Use these sites as jumping-off points and don't be afraid to reach out to a real person, such as a guidance counselor or your favorite teacher, if you're feeling overwhelmed.

A PROGRAMMER WITH AN ENGLISH DEGREE?

Scott Dafforn is the senior full-stack developer for Willo Labs. His company helps connect students with creators of digitized educational content. Historically, the educational materials market has been a source of frustration for budget-conscious students due to the high price of print-based textbooks and other learning materials. Willo Labs and other companies like it are reinventing the market around accessing information in an educational environment.

One of the interesting things about Scott is that his original plans didn't include working as a programmer. An excellent writer, he studied English in college, and when he graduated, the internet and much of the technology that goes with it were in their infancy. Still, he was drawn to programming, and it's been a great fit.

Scott Dafforn. *Courtesy of Scott Dafforn.*

Notice that when he talks about the characteristics of good IT people and his own education, he focuses on the need to think critically and to be flexible above all.

What is your current title and where do you work?

I am the senior full-stack developer for Willo Labs, a company that helps provide students with digital access to educational materials.

What are your main job duties?

I write code and develop applications and tools, and I collaborate with various teams and stakeholders to identify and design features that our platform should have. I also work with third parties to integrate with their platform(s) or help them integrate with ours.

Have you had other jobs in IT? What were they?

My first IT job was a mix of development and tier 1 support, in which I helped users understand and become comfortable with our software.

Did you start your education with the goal of being in IT?

I did not.

What is your formal educational background?

I have a bachelor of arts degree in English from Indiana University in Bloomington.

Did you get all your education at once, or did it occur over time, around jobs?

My formal education was all at once over the course of four years at college. As it relates to my career in IT, my formal education was a good foundation for thinking critically, which applies broadly to many different aspects of my job and life. The IT skills I have developed were initially self-taught, although I've learned a great deal at each job in more than twenty years in the industry.

What is a typical day like for you?

There is never a shortage of projects to work on, so the goal for each day is to make progress on those projects, whether I'm working alone or collaborating with others. Once my work is complete and tested, I submit it for peer review and, in turn, review work others have submitted. Most days include some form of communication with various customers or partners to discuss product functionality, either generally or as it relates to a specific need. Internal discussions are also frequent, through phone, e-mail, or in person, to communicate project updates, discuss customer requests, and so on. It's also common to discuss new feature design with other developers to ensure all factors are considered.

What is the most surprising thing about your job?

The sheer volume of new technology to keep track of each week, month, and year.

What are some things you really like about your job?

I enjoy the challenges presented in this line of work, and thinking creatively about solving those challenges keeps me interested.

What are some things you don't like about your job?

Technology moves at a rapid pace, with new ideas and projects truly every day. One drawback of the IT field in general, but fortunately not an issue at my actual job, is the expectation that everyone should be knowledgeable about most every technology, platform, or library, when that is simply unrealistic. Many developers subscribe to the idea that "new is better" and find themselves in a continual upgrade-and-migrate loop. This is not sustainable.

What would be your dream job within the IT field?

Full-stack development is probably the most ideal job I could have, and I've been fortunate to have had a full-stack role for nearly all of my career. Specializing in a certain area would mean sharpening those skills at the expense of broader experience and, I think, would likely also mean having a less diverse set of challenges.

What is the possible career trajectory for someone of your position? What would be an ideal job for you to be doing in five to ten years?

Career trajectory is, to an extent, the product of a person's interests. There are many facets to IT, and as people gain experience they tend to find an area of focus that interests them. The more interest and experience you have, the better suited you are to carve a niche for yourself. But while individuals can hone skills in a particular area, most businesses fail at providing avenues for professional growth. This means that employees are often provided a more traditional trajectory (for example, developer > team lead > manager > director > VP), which is problematic, because an individual's ability to develop software is no guarantee that he or she can lead others who develop software.

What are some characteristics of good IT people? What people really don't fit well in IT?

Good IT people will lack ego, listen well, enjoy challenges, be comfortable not immediately knowing answers and also owning mistakes. Anyone uncomfortable with these things will have a difficult time in most any field, not just IT.

What are some of the challenges facing the IT industry and people in it?

IT has a diversity problem on a lot of fronts, such as gender, race, and age. It's difficult to solve problems for a diverse world when the group working on those problems is predominantly men (and predominantly white).

What advice do you have for young people considering a career in information technology?

As with every field, it's important to be kind, check your ego, question your assumptions, and work hard. Be willing to accept criticism and the idea that you can't know everything. You will make mistakes, so find a way to become comfortable with that and be willing to learn from those failings. Because you can't know everything you must question everything, but do so kindly and respectfully and accept that same approach from others. Engage with your customers to truly understand their perspective and needs. Take time to get to know the people you work with, your customers, everyone. Always work hard but don't forfeit your personal life for your career, and work to become comfortable knowing when you need time away.

Making High School Count

Regardless of the career you choose, there are some basic yet important things you can do while in high school to position yourself in the most advantageous way. Remember—it's not just about having the best application; it's also about figuring out which areas of IT you actually would enjoy and which ones don't suit you. Consider these steps toward becoming a well-rounded and marketable person during your high school years:

- Volunteer at your high school or local library's help desk.

- Take as many programming and computer design and skills classes as possible during your high school career.
- Take intro classes in logic and discrete mathematics.
- Take online computer courses to enhance and expand your breadth of knowledge. You can find many free courses online.
- Use the summers to get as much experience working with computers as you can. Be comfortable using all kinds of computer software.
- Learn first aid and CPR. These important skills are useful regardless of your profession.
- Hone your communication skills in English, speech, and debate. You'll need excellent communication skills in a job where you'll have to speak with everyone from coworkers to clients and bosses.
- Consider getting certified in your areas of interest, if you have the time and money to do so.
- Volunteer in as many settings as you can.

CLASSES TO TAKE IN HIGH SCHOOL

High school is a good time to take as many electives and special-interest classes as you can, because this will give you a feeling for what you like and don't like, and it will give you experience that you can use as a stepping-stone to find internships and other positions. If your high school is on the small side, you might not have access to all the options listed here, but take what you can. It will build your portfolio and help you discover where your passions lie within the IT field.

- Basic word processing
- Computer programming
- Computer animation
- Application development
- Logic and discrete mathematics
- Computer repair
- Graphic design
- Media technology
- Video game development
- Web design
- Web programming

Taking many classes offered by your school's computer science/information technology department will also give you the opportunity to get to know the instructors who teach those classes. These are people who likely have worked, or currently work, in the fields they teach, which means they have connections and can teach you about the field outside of the classroom, as well. Note that many colleges look for comments or recommendations from teachers when considering applications. Building good relationships with your teachers can be a great way to improve your chances to receive positive recommendations.

Educational Requirements

Most people in the IT field (programmers, web developers, systems analysts and support, network engineers, security analysts and support, and so on) enter the field with a four-year bachelor's degree in something resembling computer science (information science, information technology, programming, and so on). However, it is also common and possible to be successful in the field with a two-year associate's degree, especially if you are well versed in multiple programming languages and/or are certified in several areas of expertise. The following sections cover the traditional educational requirements in detail, and then discuss a few exceptions as well.

TYPICAL DEGREES

If you want to have a successful career in the IT field, you'll need to have at least an associate's degree in a relevant field. Having a bachelor's degree will most likely place you into a better entry-level position, which may include a higher starting salary. However, with a few years of experience, the difference between these two degrees won't matter as much as whether and how well you've kept up with changes in your field.

You must have the motivation and desire to continue to learn and be educated and certified as things evolve. These are fast-paced, ever-changing fields, and you will need to stay on top of the latest trends and changes in order to be marketable and stay relevant, whether that means learning new programming languages, studying new methods for developing websites, understanding how to avoid and mitigate the latest hacks and security threats on your systems, or simply keeping up with updates and version changes in the system that you support. Some of these typical certifications will be discussed shortly, but since these change often, you should research your area of interest to find out what's happening *right now* in terms of certifications.

Let's consider the most common degrees in each of the six fields covered in this book. You'll notice here that there is some gray area in terms of actual required degrees, as well as some overlap in these fields:

- *Programmers:* These positions generally require a degree in computer science or a related field, with experience in programming languages specific to the jobs to which you're applying.
- *Technical support staff:* Depending on the type of support you provide, these positions can require anything from specific computer knowledge with no secondary degree all the way to a degree in computer science, engineering, or information science, for more technical support personnel.
- *Web developers:* Educational requirements vary here too, but it's safe to assume that you'll need programming and graphic design knowledge. For specialized positions, such as back-end web development, some employers require at least a bachelor's degree in computer science, programming, or a related field.
- *Systems analysts:* You'll fare best if you have a bachelor's degree in a computer-related field. It may also be helpful to take business courses or major in management information systems. In fact, some employers prefer applicants who have an MBA with a concentration in information systems. For more technically complex jobs, a master's degree in computer science may be more appropriate.
- *Network engineers:* Most employers require a bachelor's degree in a field related to computer or information science—degrees that focus on computer network and system administration. Because administrators work with computer hardware and equipment, a degree in computer engineering or electrical engineering is often desirable in this field.
- *Security analysts:* Similar to the systems analyst position, you'll be smart to pursue a bachelor's degree in a computer-related field, but knowledge of business administration is also desired and a plus.

"It's actually debatable whether a degree hurts or helps. Instead, think of program-ming as an apprenticeship—it's mostly about learning from your mistakes."—Gene Linetsky, software engineer and start-up founder[1]

As you can see, the actual degree type can vary greatly depending on set-ting, company setup, the technical nature of the systems at hand, and more. However, the part of your education that will be extremely important and spe-cific to your career path involves the certifications, program/system/network knowledge, and know-how you have. You won't be able to get a job as a Mi-crosoft systems administrator without a Microsoft Certified Solutions Expert (MCSE) certification, for example.

Keeping your knowledge, education, and certifications up to date is extremely important.

Each of these fields has its own languages and tools that are key to understanding and working in the field. For example, web developers need a solid understanding of HTML programming. Many employers also want them to understand programming languages such as JavaScript or SQL and have knowledge of multimedia publishing tools such as Flash. Throughout their career, as is true with all of these fields, web developers must stay up to date on new tools and computer languages as they evolve.

Certification/Training Options for Programmers

Which certifications you'll need, of course, depends on the type of programmer you want to be. Programmers generally fall within one of these categories:

- *Web programmers.* The most common languages used for web programming are XML, HTML, JavaScript, Perl 5, and PHP.[2] You don't need knowledge of and certification in all of these; instead you should pick client- or server-side programming and specialize in one area.
- *Desktop application programmers.* For Windows applications, the most common languages are C++, C# (pronounced "C-sharp"), or Visual Basic and XAML. If you're working on Mac only, Swift or Objective-C are good choices. However, be careful about limiting yourself to one operating system.
- *Library/platform/framework/core programmers.* Most programmers in this area of expertise are required to have a working knowledge and any needed certifications in Java, C, and C++.
- *System programmers.* Most programmers in this area of expertise are required to have a working knowledge and any needed certifications in C++ and Python.[3]

This list is certainly not exhaustive, and these are just examples of the types of languages and certifications you might need as you advance your career.

Certification/Training Options in Web Development

Web development is also a large field, so it makes sense to focus your attention on one of two main areas—front-end web development or back-end web development. Front-end developers are responsible for everything (or a portion thereof) sent to the client (the laptop, cloud, network, etc.). This involves knowledge of HTML, JavaScript, CSS, AngularJS, and so on. They also manage the server-side technologies that send content to the client, such as Python, Ruby, PHP, Java, and Node.js.

Back-end developers manage the interactions among the server side, the web server, and some database system. They might also work closely with user experience designers and database administrators.

Keep in mind that you won't necessarily need knowledge of every one of these languages and tools, but you will need expertise in some of the areas listed here. That said, you'll likely need advanced knowledge/skills in the following areas:

- HTML/XHTML, CSS, and JavaScript
- Server/client-side architecture
- Programming/coding/scripting in one of many server-side languages or frameworks (Perl, Python, Ruby, PHP, and so on)[4]

Certification/Training Options in Networking

If you want to be a network engineer, IT certification in networking is crucial to your success. Examples include:

- *Microsoft Network Engineer certification*—This includes the Microsoft Certified Solutions Associate (MCSA) and Microsoft Certified Solutions Expert (MCSE) credentials. Both of these require passing a series of tests.
- *Cisco Certified Network Associate (CCNA) certification*—Cisco Systems Inc. offers five levels of certifications—Entry; Associate; Professional; Expert; and Architect, which is the highest level of accreditation within the Cisco Career Certification Program.[5]

These are just two of the biggest companies that manufacture and support networks, communications products, and other high-technology offerings. They are mentioned here because they're the most well known, but there are other networking certifications that you may want to pursue.

Be sure you are aware of when your certifications expire and are ready to study and retake these exams, in order to retain certification. For example, the MCSE credential is valid for only three years, and a recertification exam is required for renewal.

Certification/Training Options for Systems and Security Analysts

There are several certification pathways related to the systems and security analyst roles. Some of the better-known companies that provide certification are:

- *Cisco*—Provides certification tracks in architect, cybersecurity operations, datacenter, security, and industrial topic areas, among others.
- *Microsoft*—Certification tracks include the MCSE, Microsoft Certified Solutions Developer (MCSD), MCSA, and Microsoft Technology Associate (MTA).
- *Oracle*—Provides certification tracks in cloud, database, systems, and enterprise management, among others.
- *IBM*—One can become an IBM certified system administrator on several IBM platforms, with tracks and tests for each path.
- *Red Hat Linux*—This open source platform provides several Linux-focused training and certification paths.

HOT TOPIC: INFORMATION SECURITY ANALYST

Because this particular field is so relevant and continues to grow, it deserves its own sidebar. Information security analysts plan and carry out security measures to protect an organization's computer networks and systems. Due to the increasing number and complexity of cyberattacks, both national and international, the responsibilities of information security analysts are continually expanding. Job outlook is much higher than the national average and median pay is near $100,000.

The same factors that make this job so in demand and well paid make it a high-stress, demanding job. It's not for everyone. But if it is something that thrills you, the future looks bright.

Some common tasks information security analysts do include:

- Monitoring their organization's networks for security breaches and investigating a violation when one occurs

- Installing and using software such as firewalls and data encryption programs to protect sensitive information
- Conducting penetration testing, which is when analysts simulate attacks to look for vulnerabilities in their systems before they can be exploited
- Developing security standards and best practices for their organization and recommending security enhancements to management or senior IT staff[6]

In terms of certifications, there are several available. Some are general information security certificates, such as the Certified Information Systems Security Professional (CISSP), while others have a narrower focus, such as penetration testing or systems auditing.[7]

To get your foot in the door, start in network administration. Many information security analysts have prior experience in an information technology department such as network or computer systems administration.

Cybersecurity and cyberattacks will continue to be a big problem for our world of interconnected computers.

> "There are, by far, more people to work and collaborate with on various projects than I imagined. It has been a terrific additional learning experience."—Amanda Gunnels, development and IT administrator

KNOWING WHAT IT TAKES TO BEAT THE ODDS

Trey Perry. *Courtesy of Trey Perry.*

Trey Perry built his information technology career in an unconventional way: He chose not to pursue a formal education, but this certainly doesn't mean he's uneducated. Instead, he's chosen a path of self-teaching and constant learning from sources outside the traditional education system.

Did he work as hard as he would have worked in college? Probably harder. His path is an uncommon one, but it's not impossible. "It's a rare angle," he says. "You've got the odds against you." But read on to see how Trey defied those odds and what he has to say about a career in information technology.

What is your current title and where do you work?

My current title is vice president of software architecture, and I work for an Austin, Texas, healthtech start-up called Wellsmith. We build a platform that collects biotelemetry from devices like glucometers, with the aim of personalizing care plans for those who have chronic disease.

What are your main job duties at Wellsmith?

We are a relatively small company with about forty people. My role is a hybrid of a principal engineer, a business manager, and a technical leader. I coordinate technical strategy and have frequent discussions with our principal investor. In effect, my job is to work on technical strategy, disseminate information as best I can, and, most important, reduce friction between various parts of the business. And in my spare time, I write code!

What are the favorite jobs you've had in the past?

Probably Bazaarvoice early on. [BazaarVoice is a company that creates software that allows users to leave product reviews on websites.] It had a unique, team-oriented, and supportive culture. I consulted for a while, and one thing about consulting is that you're able to peek into companies large and small. For me, the insight that came from that process was invaluable and taught me about many industries. Doing that, I was in touch with a lot of executives on a day-to-day level, and that was very enlightening.

What is your educational background?

Ironically, I value education very highly. In my case, I had a fledgling business, and I took an unconventional route of dropping out of college. A lot of my technical knowledge is the result of self-teaching, and I believe that in this field, regardless of your education, you need to be a strong autodidact [a person who is self-taught] or else the industry can pass you by.

Looking back, what would you say to someone who was skeptical of your decision to not pursue a formal education?

It's not everything. I've seen people with the very best of educations come out and fail. Education is valuable and can be very substantial, but it's not *everything*. My path is not one that I'd necessarily recommend to others, but there are foundational elements, and you sort of incur a debt by taking the path that I did, and you'll have some blanks to fill in later. But it also gave me a lot of hands-on experience in business and more insight as to what a customer might want. So from my perspective, my path has been a mixed bag. At the same time, I can't overstate the value of having that same experience in multiple industries and living the day-to-day responsibilities of operating a business.

I should also say that I started writing code when I was about six years old, and I was fortunate enough to have friends and family who were highly supportive of my choices.

What do you think about the importance of industry certifications and continued learning?

Ultimately, you have to be very adaptive, and you have to immerse yourself in these topics. Sometimes, that immersion does not occur in the form of, say, a vendor certification program. Instead, maybe it's simply an online course. Maybe you immerse yourself in the specifications of this product and learn by doing.

I would never discriminate a potential hire based on what acronyms appear after someone's name.

What are some things you love, and don't love, about IT?

I love that there's never a dull moment. In my role, I work with the business, people, and technology, so that's the trifecta for me.

Things I don't like about the industry as a whole is that it struggles the way many industries do: remaining compassionate, valuing people, and remaining ethical. Those are very real concerns in and around this field. In technology, we hold a lot of people's most valued secrets, all of their confidential data. There's a struggle to build and maintain that trust. I believe the industry as a whole can believe that people are assets or resources or machines, whether those people are the end users or the employees of the company. I do dislike that. That's somewhere we can do better as an industry.

What's your dream job? What would you like to be doing in ten years?

That's what I'm looking for. That's why I am where I am right now. To be a founder of another business—one that practices what it preaches, and gives back. I can see myself founding a public benefit company.

What questions should students ask to determine if IT might be right for them?

Am I adaptive? Do I handle change well? Am I determined and can I commit myself to a project even when things appear difficult? How do I handle rigidity? Those are serious questions to ask yourself. People who are adaptive, people who know when and when not to be rigid—those are people who tend to excel in this field.

Are there personality traits that are typical of people who do well in IT?

Those who are communicative and those who are compassionate make good engineering leads because you want people who can drive results while stretching people but not straining them. Also, entrepreneurial traits are extremely valuable—people who take ownership and pride in their work. This is a precision field, and if you don't have that, you won't necessarily succeed.

What challenges does the IT industry face right now?

The field is very competitive. Within the industry, there are struggles with diversity and that ethical sense we discussed earlier. Just because we have the capability to do things, should we? We've had very technical companies that have been held up as beacons in the technical industry who end up having internal challenges within their own cultures.

What advice do you have for people who, based on their gender or culture, might not feel like they're represented within the IT industry?
First, don't give up. We need diversity. This industry benefits from ideas regardless of skin color, gender, or any personal characteristics. Many technical pioneers were women, people far ahead of their time. You have as much a right as any of us to be in this industry, to be taken seriously, and you are just as intelligent.

Any other advice?
Don't limit yourself to a specific language or style. Don't stop learning. Don't stop experimenting. Don't allow technology to siphon away your passion.

Making the Most of Your Experiences

As mentioned earlier, experiences you gain out in the real world are very important pieces of the puzzle that includes your education. In other words, don't just use the time you spend in the classroom to determine if you have picked the right career path. Getting out in the real world, perhaps working in an office, will help you determine what you do and don't like and what kind of shape you want your career to take. It doesn't hurt your résumé and college applications either!

It can be hard to get your foot in the door, though. How do you get experience in the real world without having a degree or any experience to begin with? Try these approaches to gaining some much-needed experience:

- Volunteer in the IT department of a charitable or nonprofit organization that you support and ask them for a professional reference moving forward.
- Write a blog in the technical area where you want to get experience.
- Become an active contributor on technology-related discussion boards.
- Get a job as a troubleshooter, such as at Best Buy or Geek Squad.

Be sure to ask for lots of feedback from your mentors, bosses, and others. Don't be afraid to ask for advice, and be sure to have an open attitude about the information you get back.

> Maintain and cultivate professional relationships. Write thank-you notes when professionals take the time to meet with you or share their knowledge and expertise in any form, send updates about your progress and tell them where you decide to go to college, and check in occasionally. If you want to find a good mentor, you need to be a gracious and willing mentee.

NETWORKING

Because it's so important, another last word about networking. It's important to develop mentor relationships even at this stage. Remember that about 85 percent of jobs are found through personal contacts.[8] If you know someone in the field, don't hesitate to reach out. Be patient and polite, but ask for help, perspective, and guidance.

If you don't know anyone, ask your school guidance counselor to help you make connections. Or pick up the phone yourself. Reaching out with a genuine interest in knowledge and a real curiosity about the field will go a long way. You don't need a job or an internship just yet—just a connection that could blossom into a mentoring relationship. Follow these important but simple rules for the best results when networking:

- Do your homework about a potential contact, connection, university, school, or employer before you make contact. Be sure to have a general understanding of what they do and why. But don't be a know-it-all. Be open and ready to ask good questions.
- Be considerate of professionals' time and resources. Think about what they can get from you in return for mentoring or helping you.
- Speak and write using proper English. Proofread all your letters, e-mails, and even texts. Think about how you will be perceived at all times.
- Always stay positive.
- Show your passion for the subject matter.

Summary

In this chapter, you learned even more about what it's like to work in the IT field. This chapter discussed the educational requirements of these different areas, from college degrees to licensing to master's degrees. You also learned about getting experience in the field before you enter college as well as during the educational process. At this time, you should have a good idea of the educational requirements for your area of interest. You hopefully even contemplated some questions about what kind of educational career path fits your strengths, timetable, and wallet. Are you starting to picture your career plan? If not, that's okay, as there's still time.

Remember that no matter which area of IT you pursue, these technologies continually change. You must stay up to date on the latest changes and developments, keep your certifications current, and meet the continuing education requirements. This is very important in the IT field. Advances in computers are constant, and it's vitally important that you keep apprised of what's happening in your field. The bottom line is that you need to have a lifelong love of learning to succeed in this field.

> "The thought is, 'Okay, I'll learn this particular language and then that's the language I'll work in for the rest of my life.' I learned very early that that's not the case, that you have to continue to learn quite a bit."—Cary Chandler, chief operations officer

Chapter 3 goes into a lot more detail about pursing the best educational path. The chapter covers how to find the best value for your education and includes discussion about financial aid and scholarships. At the end of chapter 3, you should have a much clearer view of the educational landscape and how and where you fit in.

3

Pursuing the Education Path

*W*hen it comes time to start looking at colleges, universities, or postsecondary schools, many high schoolers tend to freeze up at the enormity of the job ahead of them. This chapter will help break down this process for you so it won't seem so daunting.

It's true that finding the right college or learning institution is an important one, and it's a big step toward achieving your career goals and dreams. The last chapter covered the various educational requirements of the IT professions, which means you should now be ready to find the right institution of learning. This isn't always just a process of finding the very best school that you can afford and can be accepted into, although that might end up being your path. It should also be about finding the right fit so that you can have the best possible experience during your post–high school years.

But here's the truth of it all: Postsecondary schooling isn't just about getting a degree. It's about learning how to be an adult, managing your life and your responsibilities, being exposed to new experiences, growing as a person, and otherwise moving toward becoming an adult who contributes to society. College—in whatever form it takes for you—offers you an opportunity to actually become an interesting person with perspective on the world and empathy and consideration for people other than yourself, if you let it.

An important component of how successful you will be in college is finding the right fit, the right school that brings out the best in you and challenges you at different levels. I know—no pressure, right? Just as with finding the right profession, your ultimate goal should be to match your personal interests, goals, and personality with the college's goals and perspective. For example, small liberal arts colleges have a much different feel and philosophy than Big 10 state schools. And rest assured that all this advice applies even if you're planning on attending community college or another postsecondary school.

Don't worry, though: In addition to these soft skills, this chapter does dive into the nitty-gritty of how to find the best school, no matter what you want to do. In the IT field specifically, attending a respected program is important to future success, and that is covered in detail in this chapter.

WHAT IS A GAP YEAR?

Taking a year off between high school and college, often called a gap year, is normal, perfectly acceptable, and almost required in many countries around the world. It is becoming increasingly acceptable in the United States as well. Even Malia Obama, President Obama's daughter, did it. Because the cost of college has gone up dramatically, it literally pays for you to know going in what you want to study, and a gap year—well spent—can do lots to help you answer that question.

Some great ways to spend your gap year include joining organizations such as the Peace Corps or AmeriCorps, enrolling in a mountaineering program or other gap year–styled program, backpacking across Europe or other countries on the cheap (be safe and bring a friend), finding a volunteer organization that furthers a cause you believe in or that complements your career aspirations, joining a Road Scholar program (see www.roadscholar.org), teaching English in another country (more information available at www.gooverseas.com/blog/best-countries-for-seniors-to-teach-english-abroad), or working and earning money for college!

Many students find that they get much more out of college when they have a year to mature and to experience the real world. The American Gap Year Association reports from alumni surveys that students who take gap years show improved civic engagement, improved college graduation rates, and improved GPAs in college.[1] You can use your gap year to explore and solidify your thoughts and plans about an IT career, as well as add impressive experiences to your college application.

See the association's website at https://gapyearassociation.org for lots of advice and resources if you're considering this potentially life-altering experience.

Finding a School That Fits Your Personality

Before looking at the details of good schools for a career in IT, it will behoove you to take some time to consider what type of school will be best for you.

Answering questions like the ones that follow can help you narrow your search and focus on a smaller set of choices. Write your answers to these questions down somewhere where you can refer to them often, such as in the Notes app on your phone:

- *Size:* Does the size of the school matter to you? Colleges and universities range in size from five hundred or fewer students to twenty-five thousand students.
- *Community location:* Would you prefer to be in a rural area, a small town, a suburban area, or a large city? How important is the location of the school in the larger world?
- *Distance from home:* Will you live at home to save money? If not, how far away from home—in terms of hours or miles away—do you want/ are you willing to go?
- *Housing options:* What kind of housing would you prefer? Dorms, off-campus apartments, and private homes are all common options.
- *Student body:* How would you like the student body to look? Think about coed versus all-male and all-female settings, as well as ethnic and racial diversity, how many students are part-time versus full-time, and the percentage of commuter students.
- *Academic environment:* Which majors are offered, and at which degree levels? Research the student-faculty ratio. Are the classes taught often by actual professors or more often by the teaching assistants? How many internships does the school typically provide to students? Are independent study or study abroad programs available in your area of interest?
- *Financial aid availability/cost:* Does the school provide ample opportunities for scholarships, grants, work-study programs, and the like? Does cost play a role in your options? (For most people, it does.)
- *Support services:* How strong are the school's academic and career placement counseling services?
- *Social activities and athletics:* Does the school offer clubs that you are interested in? Which sports are offered? Are scholarships available?
- *Specialized programs:* Does the school offer honors programs or programs for veterans or students with disabilities or special needs?

"There are many facets to IT, and as people gain experience they tend to find an area of focus that interests them. The more interest and experience you have, the better suited you are to carve a niche for yourself."—Scott Dafforn, senior full-stack developer

Not all of these questions are going to be important to you, and that's fine. Be sure to make note of aspects that don't matter as much to you. You might change your mind as you visit colleges, but it's important to make note of where you are to begin with.

U.S. News & World Report puts it best when it reports that the college that fits you best is one that:

- Offers a degree that matches your interests and needs
- Provides a style of instruction that matches the way you like to learn

Be sure you find the type of postsecondary school that fits your needs and budget.

- Provides a level of academic rigor to match your aptitude and preparation
- Offers a community that feels like home to you
- Values you for what you do well[2]

According to the National Center for Education Statistics (NCES), which is part of the US Department of Education, six years after entering college for an undergraduate degree, only 60 percent of students have graduated.[3]

By the same token, it's never been more important to get your degree. College graduates with a bachelor's degree typically earn 66 percent more than those with only a high school diploma and are also far less likely to face unemployment.[4] Also, over the course of a lifetime, the average worker with a bachelor's degree will earn approximately $1 million more than a worker without a postsecondary education.[5]

Hopefully, this section has impressed upon you the importance of finding the right college fit. Take some time to paint a mental picture of the kind of university or school setting that will best meet your needs. Then read on for specifics about the different IT degrees.

A ONE-WOMAN IT SHOP IN A SMALL (AND BUSY) COMPANY

Amanda Gunnels is the development and IT administrator for a property development company in Cleveland. Her company builds and markets apartment complexes and retail stores in the Cleveland area. As a result, one of her tasks is to build websites that accurately show users the types of apartments they could live in. She also has to make sure that the site correctly ties into the engine that shows how many apartments are available as well as the tool that helps set up appointments for interested prospective renters.

And that's just for the company's various websites. As the IT administrator, she also needs to make sure that the technology for all of the company' employees is running smoothly. She's a one-woman IT shop within a small but active company.

Amanda Gunnels. *Courtesy of Amanda Gunnels.*

As you read through her interview, one of the themes you'll see is that she expects—and embraces—constant change. This change comes from software tools, the needs of her internal users, her company's customers, and the people she works with every day.

What is your current title and where do you work?

I work as the development and IT administrator for VVXZ Development, a residential property development company with headquarters in Cleveland, Ohio.

What are your main job duties?

My main duties include web design and development, building and maintaining software applications, and managing our cloud computing resources.

Have you had other jobs in IT? What were they?

I independently contracted jobs for web design and development prior to my current position. I also found it to be incredibly important and fulfilling to donate my services to nonprofits at least once a year.

Did you start your education with the goal of being in IT?

Yes.

What is your formal educational background?

I have taken courses in computer and software engineering at Case Western Reserve University.

Do you have any industry-specific certifications?

My certifications include Java OOP (Object-Oriented Programming) and Full Stack Language Certifications.

Did you get all your education at once, or did it occur over time, around jobs?

It was a process of working and going to school for what seemed like an eternity. The commitment to accomplish and excel in these programs paid off. I can now truly say, "I love what I do."

What is a typical day like for you?

Every day is different. In a nutshell, I handle pop-up emergencies with my fellow employees, systems, and applications. Each day is about detail in monitoring our current published pages as well as planning and designing new sites.

What is the most surprising thing about your job?

There are, by far, more people to work and collaborate with on various projects than I imagined. It has been a terrific additional learning experience.

What are some things you really like about your job?

My favorite is writing a full-stack program, or refacing an existing page. Little by little, bit by bit, it is enthralling to see each component build, connect, and operate through the testing process until it becomes a beautiful, published web page.

What are some things you don't like about your job?

It is occasionally a requirement to bend my hours either before or after normal business hours in order to complete projects and not disrupt everyone else's ability to operate. This doesn't happen all too often, but it can make for an exhausting day. Nonetheless, it doesn't distract me from feeling incredibly happy to be in this field of choice.

What would be your dream job within the IT field?

I would love to establish a company that catered to nonprofit organizations.

What is the possible career trajectory for someone of your position? What would be an ideal job for you to be doing in five to ten years?

I work in a small company and handle all of our IT affairs and responsibilities. At this juncture, for me personally, I am awaiting more technical advances and languages to enter into the picture. I see continued education and growth!

What are some characteristics of good IT people? What people really don't fit well in IT?

- Part 1: Patience. Patience is extremely important. Everyone has a forte and not all are in technology. When dealing with people who have limited knowledge or experience with technology, it is imperative to remain calm and be informative. Additionally, the biggest part of software engineering and development is that things break. Often. You just keep writing and trying until your program responds—and when it does, it feels like the greatest accomplishment every time!
- Part 2: You must be a person who enjoys fine and precise details. Troubleshooting is a frequent occurrence in technology, no matter what branch you choose to be in.

What are some of the challenges facing the IT industry and people in it?

There is a growing interest in purchasing templates instead of designing full-stack programs. This cuts the need for people and slices earnings over time, dramatically.

What advice do you have for young people—and especially girls and young women—considering a career in information technology?

Always plan ahead. There are a plethora of guides, training, and low-cost online courses you can take. Try it out. Play around with things. See what you like the best. There is a whole world with vast amounts of possibilities. Believe in yourself, be true to yourself, and go get what you want. I left from already having an established career path and chose to do a 180. I regret nothing. I love and have a genuine passion for what I do.

For young women, there are groups you can become a part of and different ways of networking. One example is https://www.womenwhocode.com/.

Get involved. It is good to surround yourself with people of all levels in technology so you can be both helped and helpful.

Honing Your Degree Plan

This section outlines the different approaches you can take to get a degree that will help you land your dream job in information technology, whether it be as a web developer, programmer, security analyst, network engineer, or something related to one of these. Let's start by reviewing what we learned in chapter 1 about salaries in these fields.

> "I've seen people with the very best of educations come out and fail. Education is valuable and can be very substantial, but it's not *everything*."—Trey Perry, VP of software architecture

Salary Data

Recall that the US Bureau of Labor Statistics reports that the average pay for IT professionals breaks down as follows, based on 2017 data:

- Network support specialists had a median income of $62,340; computer user support specialists had a median wage of $50,210.

- The median yearly income for computer programmers was $82,200.
- Network engineers made $82,050 annually.
- Security analysts made $98,350 annually.
- Web developers made $69,430 yearly.

You can check the Bureau of Labor Statistics website at www.bls.gov for updated salary information. Also, keep in mind that these are averages across the country. If you live in the Midwest or the South, where the cost of living is lower, you'll likely make less than if you live on either coast. This is true regardless of profession.

RELEVANT DEGREE PATHS TO CONSIDER

As you've no doubt learned if you've read this far into the book, the IT umbrella has many varied but related professions within it. No matter which area you want to focus on, having at least a two-year associate's degree in computer science or information science is rapidly becoming a requirement to get most IT jobs. Consider these points:

- As an associate's degree is a two-year process, it's less expensive and takes less time. Many web developers and tech support personnel start their careers with associate's degrees in computer science or information science. Once you are hired, your employer might pay for you to get your bachelor's degree.
- If you want to enter the workforce as a network engineer, systems analyst, or security analyst, you'll likely need a four-year bachelor's degree. This could be in computer or information science, of course, or maybe even in mathematics, information systems, or engineering.

So what does the typical computer science degree require of you? Typical computer science students will be required to take the following classes before moving into specifics related to their area of choice:

- Lots of math, including calculus
- Mathematical logic
- Physics
- Electronics
- Statistics and probability

In addition, a typical computer science degree will offer courses on the following subjects:

- Applied computer science
- Coding
- Computer networking
- Microsoft certification
- Operating systems
- Programming languages
- Software engineering
- Database design
- Data logic and management

These are just examples of the courses you will take to earn your degree. Be sure to check the curricula of the schools you're considering attending for more specific information.

Starting Your College Search

If you're currently in high school and you are serious about working in the IT field, start by finding four to five schools in a realistic location (for you) that offer degrees in computer science. Not every school near you or that you have an initial interest in will offer the degree you desire, so narrow your choices accordingly. With that said, consider attending a public university in your resident state, if possible, which will save you lots of money. Private institutions don't typically discount resident student tuition costs.

Be sure you research the basic GPA and SAT or ACT requirements of each school as well.

For students applying to associate's degree programs or higher, most advisers recommend that students take both the ACT and the SAT tests during the spring of their junior year. (The ACT test is generally considered more weighted in science, so take that into consideration.) You can retake these tests and use your highest score, so be sure to leave time for a retake early in your senior year if needed. You want your best score to be available to all the schools you're applying to by January of your senior year, which will also enable your score to be considered with any scholarship applications. Keep in mind that these are general timelines—be sure to check the exact deadlines and calendars of the schools to which you're applying!

Once you have found four to five schools in a realistic location for you that offer the degree you want to pursue, spend some time on their websites studying the requirements for admission. Most universities list the average stats for the last class accepted to the program. Important factors in weighing your decision about what schools to apply to should include whether or not you meet the requirements, your chances of getting in (but shoot high!), tuition costs, availability of scholarships and grants, location, and the school's reputation and licensure/graduation rates.

The importance of these characteristics will depend on your grades and test scores, your financial resources, and other personal factors. You want to find a university with a good computer science program that also matches your academic rigor and practical needs.

THE MOST PERSONAL OF PERSONAL STATEMENTS

The personal statement you include with your application to college is extremely important, especially if your GPA and SAT/ACT scores are on the border of what is typically accepted. Write something that is thoughtful and conveys your understanding of the IT profession, as well as your desire to work in the information technology world. Why are you uniquely qualified? Why are you a good fit for the university and program? These essays should be highly personal (the *personal* in personal statement). Will the admissions professionals who read it—along with hundreds of others—come away with a snapshot of who you really are and what you are passionate about?

Look online for some examples of good personal statements, which will give you a feel for what works. Be sure to check your specific school for length guidelines, format requirements, and any other guidelines you are expected to follow. Most important, make sure your passion for your potential career comes through—although make sure it is also genuine.

And of course, be sure to proofread it several times and ask a professional (such as your school writing center or your local library services) to proofread it as well.

What's It Going to Cost You?

So, the bottom line: What will your education end up costing you? Of course, this depends on many factors, including the type and length of degree you pursue, where you attend (in state or not, private or public institution), how much in scholarships or financial aid you're able to obtain, your family or personal income, and many other factors. The College Entrance Examination Board tracks and summarizes financial data from colleges and universities all over the United States. (You can find more information at www.collegeboard.org.) A sample of the most recent data is shown in table 3.1.

Keep in mind that these are averages and reflect the published prices, not the net prices (see the sidebar "The All-Important Net Cost"). As an example of net cost, in 2018–2019, full-time, in-state students at a public four-year college must cover an average of about $14,900 in tuition and fees and room and board after grant aid and tax benefits, in addition to paying for books, supplies, and other living expenses.

If you read more specific data about a particular university or find averages in your particular area of interest, you should assume those numbers are closer to reality than these, as they are more specific. This data helps to show you the ballpark figures.

Table 3.1. Average Yearly Tuition, Fees, and Room and Board for Full-Time Undergraduates

Year	Public 4 Year, In State	Public 4 Year, Out of State	Private Nonprofit
2017–2018	$21,400	$38,420	$48,380
2018–2019	$21,370	$38,570	$48,500

Source: College Entrance Examination Board website, https://trends.collegeboard.org/college-pricing/figures-tables/tuition-fees-room-and-board-over-time

THE ALL-IMPORTANT NET COST

The actual, final price (or net price) that you'll pay for a specific college is the difference between the published price (tuition and fees) to attend that college, minus any grants, scholarships, and education tax benefits you receive (money you don't have to pay back). This difference can be significant. In 2015–2016, the average published price of in-state tuition and fees for public four-year colleges was about $9,139 (*not* including room and board), but the average net price of in-state tuition and fees for public four-year colleges was only about $3,030.[6]

Most college websites have net price calculators on their websites that use the information you enter to come up with a personalized estimate of how much gift aid that particular college may offer you—and consequently what it will really cost you to attend. (So the net price is a personal number that varies from student to student. It considers factors like financial need, academic performance, and athletic talent.) The net price is the best number to use when you're comparing different university costs, because it takes into account each school's scholarships and grants, which can vary significantly from school to school. By comparing net prices instead of the published prices, you might find out that you can actually afford the school you thought was too expensive!

Generally speaking, there is about a 3 percent annual increase in tuition and associated costs to attend college. In other words, if you are expecting to attend college two years after this data was collected, you need to add approximately 6 percent to these numbers. Keep in mind that this assumes no financial aid or scholarships of any kind (so it's not the net cost).

This chapter discusses finding the most affordable path to get the degree you want. Later in this chapter, you'll also learn how to prime the pumps and get as much money for college as you can.

Touring the campus and talking to current students is really important.

MAKE THE MOST OF SCHOOL VISITS

If it's at all practical and feasible, you should visit the schools you're considering. To get a real feel for any college or school, you need to walk around the campus and buildings, spend some time in the common areas where students hang out, and sit in on a few classes. You can also sign up for campus tours, which are typically given by current students. This is another good way to see the school and ask questions of someone who knows. Be sure to visit the specific school/building that covers your intended major as well. Websites and brochures won't be able to convey that intangible feeling you'll get from a visit.

Make a list of questions that are important to you before you visit. In addition to the questions listed earlier in this chapter, consider these questions as well:

- What is the makeup of the current freshman class? Is the campus diverse?
- What is the meal plan like? What are the food options?
- Where do most of the students hang out between classes? (Be sure to visit this area.)

- How long does it take to walk from one end of the campus to the other?
- What types of transportation are available for students? Does campus security provide escorts to cars, dorms, and other on-campus destinations at night?

To prepare for your visit and make the most of it, consider these tips and words of advice:

- Listen and take notes.
- Don't interrupt.
- Be positive and energetic.
- Make eye contact when someone speaks directly to you.
- Ask questions.
- Thank people for their time.

Before you go:

- Be sure to do some research. At the very least, spend some time on the college's website. You may find your questions are addressed adequately there first.
- Make a list of questions.
- Arrange to meet with a professor in your area of interest or to visit the specific school.
- Be prepared to answer questions about yourself and why you are interested in this school.
- Dress in neat, clean, and casual clothes. Avoid overly wrinkled clothing or anything with stains.

Finally, be sure to send thank-you notes or e-mails after the visit is over. Remind recipients when you visited the campus and thank them for their time.

Financial Aid and Student Loans

Finding the money to attend college—whether a two- or four-year college program, an online program, or a vocational career college—can seem overwhelm-

Paying for college can take a creative mix of grants, scholarships, and loans, but you can find your way with some help!

ing. But you can do it if you have a plan before you actually start applying to colleges. If you get into your top-choice university, don't let the sticker price turn you away. Financial aid can come from many different sources, and it's available to cover all different kinds of costs you'll encounter during your years in college, including tuition, fees, books, housing, and food.

The good news is that universities more often offer incentive or tuition discount aid to encourage students to attend. The market is often more competitive in the favor of the student, and colleges and universities are responding by offering more generous aid packages to a wider range of students than they used to. Here are some basic tips and pointers about the financial aid process:

- Apply for financial aid during your senior year. You must fill out the Free Application for Student Aid (FAFSA) form, which can be filed starting October 1 of your senior year until June of the year you graduate.[7] Because the amount of available aid is limited, it's best to apply as soon as you possibly can. See https://studentaid.ed.gov/sa/fafsa to get started.

- Be sure to compare and contrast the deals you get from different schools. There is room to negotiate with universities. The first offer for aid may not be the best you'll get.
- Wait until you receive all offers from your top schools and then use this information to negotiate with your top choice to see if it will match or beat the best aid package you received.
- To be eligible to keep and maintain your financial aid package, you must meet certain grade/GPA requirements. Be sure you are very clear about these academic expectations and keep up with them.
- You must reapply for federal aid every year.

Watch out for scholarship scams! You should never be asked to pay to submit the FAFSA form (*free* is in its name) or be required to pay a lot to find appropriate aid and scholarships. These are free services. If an organization promises you you'll get aid or that you have to "act now or miss out," these are both warning signs of a less-than-reputable organization.

You should also be careful with your personal information to avoid identity theft as well. Simple things like closing and exiting your browser after visiting sites where you entered personal information goes a long way. Don't share your student aid ID number with anyone, either.

It's important to understand the different forms of financial aid that are available to you. That way, you'll know how to apply for different kinds and get the best financial aid package that fits your needs and strengths. The two main categories that financial aid falls under are gift aid, which doesn't have to be repaid, and self-help aid, which includes loans that must be repaid and work-study funds that are earned. The next sections cover the various types of financial aid that fit into one of these areas.

GRANTS

Grants typically are awarded to students who have financial need, but can also be used in the areas of athletics, academics, demographics, veteran support, and special talents. They do not have to be paid back. Grants can come from federal agencies, state agencies, specific universities, and private organizations. Most federal and state grants are based on financial need. Examples of grants are the Pell Grant and the SMART Grant.

SCHOLARSHIPS

Scholarships are merit-based aid that does not have to be paid back. They are typically awarded based on academic excellence or some other special talent, such as music or art. Scholarships can also be athletic-based, minority-based, aid for women, and so forth. These are typically not awarded by federal or state governments, but instead come from the specific school you applied to as well as private and nonprofit organizations.

Be sure to reach out directly to the financial aid officers of the schools you want to attend. These people are great contacts who can lead you to many more sources of scholarships and financial aid. Visit GoCollege's Financial Aid Finder at www.gocollege.com/goscholarshipsearch for lots more information about how scholarships in general work.

LOANS

Many types of loans are available, especially for students to pay for their post-secondary education. However, the important thing to remember here is that loans must be paid back, with interest. (This is the extra cost of borrowing the money and is usually a percentage of the amount you borrow.) Be sure you understand the interest rate you will be charged. Is this fixed or will it change over time? Are payments on the loan and interest deferred until you graduate (meaning you don't have to begin paying it off until after you graduate)? Is the loan subsidized (meaning the federal government pays the interest until you graduate)? These are all points you need to be clear about before you sign on the dotted line.

There are many types of loans offered to students, including need-based loans, non-need-based loans, state loans, and private loans. Two very reputable federal loans are the Perkins Loan and the Direct Stafford Loan. For more information about student loans, visit https://bigfuture.collegeboard.org/pay-for-college/loans/types-of-college-loans.

FEDERAL WORK-STUDY

The US federal work-study program provides part-time jobs for undergraduate and graduate students with financial need so they can earn money to pay for educational expenses. The focus of such work is on community service work and work related to a student's course of study. Not all schools participate in this program, so be sure to check with the financial aid office at any schools you are considering if this is something you are counting on. The sooner you apply, the more likely you will get the job you desire and be able to benefit from the program, as funds are limited. See https://studentaid.ed.gov/sa/types/work-study for more information about this opportunity.

Making High School Count

If you are still in high school or middle school, there are many things you can do now to nurture your interest in informational technology and set yourself up for success. Consider these tips for your remaining years:

- Work on listening well and speaking and communicating clearly. Work on writing clearly and effectively.
- Learn how to learn. This means keeping an open mind, asking questions, asking for help when you need it, taking good notes, and doing your homework.
- Plan a daily homework schedule and keep up with it. Have a consistent, quiet place to study.
- Talk about your career interests with friends, family, and counselors. They may have connections to people in your community whom you can shadow or who will mentor you.
- Try new interests and activities, especially during your first two years of high school.
- Be involved in extracurricular activities that truly interest you and say something about who you are and who you want to be.

Kids are under so much pressure these days to do it all, but you should think about working smarter rather than harder. If you are involved in things

Remember to take care of yourself and to enjoy the journey to adulthood!

you enjoy, your educational load won't seem like such a burden. Be sure to take time for self-care, such as sleep, unscheduled downtime, and activities that you find fun and energizing. See chapter 4 for more ways to relieve and avoid stress.

Summary

This chapter looked at all the aspects of college and postsecondary schooling that you'll want to consider as you move forward. Remember that finding the right fit is especially important, as it increases the chances that you'll stay in school and finish your degree or program—and have an amazing experience while you're there.

In this chapter, you learned a little about what a typical computer science degree will require of you. You also learned about how to get the best education for the best deal. You learned a little about scholarships and financial aid, how the SAT and ACT tests work, and how to write a unique personal statement that eloquently expresses your passions.

Use this chapter as a jumping-off point to dig deeper into your particular area of interest, but don't forget these important points:

- Take the SAT and ACT tests early in your junior year so you have time to take them again if you need to. Most schools automatically accept the highest scores (but be sure to check your specific schools' policies).
- Don't underestimate how important school visits are, especially in the pursuit of finding the right academic fit. Come prepared to ask questions not addressed on the school's website or in the literature.
- Your personal statement is a very important piece of your application that can set you apart from other applicants. Take the time and energy needed to make it unique and compelling.
- Don't assume you can't afford a school based on the sticker price. Many schools offer great scholarships and aid to qualified students. It doesn't hurt to apply. This advice especially applies to minorities, veterans, and students with disabilities.
- Don't lose sight of the fact that it's important to pursue a career that you enjoy, are good at, and are passionate about! You'll be a happier person if you do so.

> "Believe in yourself, be true to yourself, and go get what you want. I left from already having an established career path and chose to do a 180. I regret nothing. I love what I do."—Amanda Gunnels, development and IT administrator

At this point, your career goals and aspirations should be jelling. At the very least, you should have a plan for finding out more information. And don't forget about networking, which was covered in more detail in chapter 2. Remember to do the research about the school or degree program before you reach out and especially before you visit. Faculty and staff find students who ask challenging questions much more impressive than those who ask questions that can be answered by spending ten minutes on the school's website.

Chapter 4 goes into detail about the next steps—writing a résumé and cover letter, interviewing well, follow-up communications, and more. This information is not just for college grads; you can use it to secure internships, volunteer positions, summer jobs, and other opportunities. In fact, the sooner you can hone these communication skills, the better off you'll be in the professional world.

4

Writing Your Résumé and Interviewing

No matter which area of IT you aspire to work in, having a well-written résumé and impeccable interviewing skills will help you reach your ultimate goals. This chapter provides some helpful tips and advice to build the best résumé and cover letter, how to interview well with all your prospective employers, and how to communicate effectively and professionally at all times. The advice in this chapter isn't just for people entering the workforce full-time, either; it can help you score that internship or summer job or help you give a great college interview to impress the admissions office.

After discussing how to write your résumé, the chapter looks at important interviewing skills that you can build and develop over time. The chapter also has some tips for dealing successfully with stress, which is an inevitable by-product of a busy life.

Writing Your Résumé

If you're a teen writing a résumé for your first job, you likely don't have a lot of work experience under your belt yet. Because of this limited work experience, you need to include classes and coursework that are related to the job you're seeking, as well as any school activities and volunteer experience you have. While you are writing your résumé, you might discover some talents and recall some activities you did that you forgot about but that are important to add. Think about volunteer work, side jobs you've held (help desk work, tutoring, troubleshooting your neighbor's computer, etc.), and the like. A good approach at this point in your career is to build a functional résumé, which focuses on your abilities rather than work experience, and it's discussed in detail next.

PARTS OF A RÉSUMÉ

The functional résumé is the best approach when you don't have a lot of pertinent work experience, as it is written to highlight your abilities rather than your experience. (The other, perhaps more common, type of résumé is called the chronological résumé, which lists a person's accomplishments in chronological order, most recent jobs listed first.) This section breaks down and discusses the functional résumé in greater detail.

Here are the essential parts of your résumé, listed from the top down:

- *Heading:* This should include your name, address, and contact information, including phone, e-mail, and website if you have one. This information is typically centered at the top of the page.
- *Objective:* This is one sentence that tells the specific employer what kind of position you are seeking. This should be modified to be specific to each potential employer.
- *Education:* Always list your most recent school or program first. Include date of completion (or expected date of graduation), degree or certificate earned, and the institution's name and address. Include workshops, seminars, and related classes here as well.
- *Skills:* Skills include computer literacy, leadership skills, organizational skills, and time-management skills. Be specific in this area when possible, and tie your skills to working in the IT field when appropriate.
- *Activities:* Activities can be related to skills. Perhaps an activity listed here helped you develop a skill listed above. This section can be combined with the Skills section, but it's often helpful to break these apart if you have enough substantive things to say in both areas. Examples include camps, sports teams, leadership roles, community service work, clubs and organizations, and so on, as well as any activities that involved working on computers.
- *Experience:* If you don't have any actual work experience that's relevant, you might consider skipping this section. However, you can list summer, part-time, and volunteer jobs you've held, again focusing on work related to IT.
- *Interests:* This section is optional, but it's a chance to include special talents and interests. Keep it short, factual, and specific.

- *References:* It's best to say that references are available on request. If you do list actual contacts, list no more than three and make sure you inform your contacts that they might be contacted.

The first three parts above are pretty much standard, but the others can be creatively combined or developed to maximize your abilities and experience. These are not set-in-stone sections that every résumé must have.

If you're still not seeing the big picture here, it's helpful to look at student and part-time résumé examples online to see how others have approached this process. Search for "functional résumé examples" to get a look at some examples.

RÉSUMÉ-WRITING TIPS

Regardless of your situation and why you're writing the résumé, there are some basic tips and techniques you should use:

- Keep it short and simple. This includes using a simple, standard font and format. Using one of the résumé templates included in your word processor software can be a great way to start.

The online job application process requires patience and attention to detail.

- Use simple language. Keep it to one page.
- Highlight your academic achievements, such as a high GPA (above 3.5) or academic awards. If you have taken classes related to the job you're interviewing for, list those briefly as well.
- Emphasize your extracurricular activities, internships, and the like. These could include camps, clubs, sports, tutoring, or volunteer work. Use these activities to show your skills, interests, and abilities.
- Use action verbs, such as *led, created, taught, ran,* and *developed.*
- Be specific and give examples.
- Always be honest.
- Include leadership roles and experience.
- Edit and proofread at least twice, and have someone else do the same. Ask a professional (such as your school writing center or your local library services) to proofread it for you also. Don't forget to run spell check.
- Include a cover letter (discussed in the next section).

THE COVER LETTER

Every résumé you send out should include a cover letter. This can be the most important part of your job search because it's often the first thing that potential employers read. By including a cover letter, you're showing employers that you took the time to learn about their organization and address them personally. This goes a long way to show that you're interested in the position.

Be sure to call the company or verify on the website the name and title of the person to whom you should address the letter. This letter should be brief. Introduce yourself and begin with a statement that will grab the person's attention. Keep in mind that employers will potentially receive hundreds of résumés and cover letters for every open position.

Like the résumé, you have a little room to be creative with a cover letter, but it should contain the following parts in order, from top to bottom:

- Your name, address, phone number, and e-mail address
- The current date
- The recipient's name, title, company name, and company address
- Salutation

- Body (usually one to three paragraphs)
- Closing (your signature and name)

The body portion of the cover letter should mention how you heard about the position, something extra about you that will interest the potential employer, practical skills you can bring to the position, and past experience related to the job. You should apply the facts outlined in your résumé to the job to which you're applying.

Your cover letter should be as short as possible while still conveying a sense of who you are and why you want this particular job or to work for this particular company. Do your research into the company and include some details about the company in your letter—this demonstrates that you cared enough to take the time to learn something about the company.

Always try to find out the name and title of the person who will be handling your application. This is usually listed in the job posting, but if not, taking the time to track it down yourself on the company website can pay off. Think about it: Imagine that you read nine cover letters addressed "Dear Sir or Madam" before reading a tenth addressed to you using your name. Wouldn't that one catch your attention?

Here are a few more things to keep in mind when writing your cover letter:

- As with the résumé, proofread it many times and have others proofread it too. You don't want a potential employer to discard a great letter you worked so hard on just because you forgot to finish a sentence or made some clumsy mistake.
- Use "Mr." for male names and "Ms." for female names in your salutation. If you can't figure out the gender of the person who will be handling your application from the name, just use the person's full name ("Dear Jamie Smith").
- As much as possible, connect the specific qualifications the company is looking for with your skill set and experience. The closer you can make yourself resemble the ideal candidate described in the ad, the more likely you will be called for an interview.

- If you're lacking one or more qualifications the employer is looking for, just ignore it. Don't call attention to it by pointing it out or making an excuse. Leave it up to the employer to decide how important it is and whether to still call you in for an interview. Your other skills and experience may more than make up for any one deficit.
- You want to seem eager, competent, helpful, and dependable. Think about things from the employer's point of view. Focus your letter much more on what you can do for the employer than on what the employer can do for you. Be someone that *you* would want to hire.
- For more advice on cover letters, check out the free guide by Resume Genius at https://resumegenius.com/cover-letters-the-how-to-guide.

RÉSUMÉS, COVER LETTERS, AND ONLINE JOB APPLICATIONS

Résumés and cover letters are holdovers from the era before the internet—even from before personal computers. They were designed to be typed on paper and delivered through the mail. Obviously these days much of the job application process has moved online. Nevertheless, the essential concepts communicated by the résumé and cover letter haven't changed. Most employers who accept online applications ask that you either e-mail or upload your résumé.

Those who ask you to e-mail your résumé will specify which document formats they accept. The Adobe Acrobat PDF format is often preferred, because many programs can display a PDF (including web browsers), and documents in this format are mostly uneditable—that is, they can't easily be changed. In these cases, you attach the résumé to your e-mail, and your e-mail itself becomes the cover letter. The same principles of the cover letter discussed in this section apply to this e-mail, except you skip the addresses and date at the top and begin directly with the salutation.

Some employers direct you to a section on their website where you can upload your résumé. In these cases, it may not be obvious where your cover letter content should go. Look for a text box labeled something like "Personal Statement" or "Additional Information." Those are good places to add whatever you would normally write in a cover letter. If there doesn't seem to be anywhere like that, see if there is an e-mail link to the hiring manager or whoever will be reading your résumé. Go ahead and send your cover e-mail to this address, mentioning that you have uploaded your résumé (again omitting the addresses and date at the top of your cover letter). Try to use the person's name if it has been given.

If you are e-mailing your cover letter instead of printing it out, you'll need to pay particular attention to the subject line of your e-mail. Be sure that it is specific to the position you are applying for. In all cases, it's really important to follow the employer's instructions about how to submit your cover letter and résumé. Generally speaking, sending a PDF rather than editable documents is preferred. Most word processing programs have an option under the Save command that allows you to save your work as a PDF.

EFFECTIVELY HANDLING STRESS

As you're forging ahead with your life plans—whether it's college, a full-time job, or even a gap year—you might find that these decisions feel very important and heavy and that the stress is difficult to deal with. This is completely normal. Try these simple techniques to relieve stress:

- Take deep breaths in and out. Try this for thirty seconds. You'll be amazed at how it can help.
- Close your eyes and clear your mind.
- Go scream at the passing subway car. Or lock yourself in a closet and scream. Or scream into a pillow. For some people, this can really help.
- Keep the issue in perspective. Any decision you make now can be changed if it doesn't work out.

Want to know how to avoid stress altogether? It is surprisingly simple. Of course, simple doesn't always mean easy, but these ideas are basic and make sense based on what we know about the human body:

- Get enough sleep.
- Eat healthy.
- Get exercise.
- Go outside.
- Schedule downtime.
- Connect with friends and family.

The bottom line is that you need to take time for self-care. There will always be stress in life, but how you deal with it makes all the difference. This only becomes more important as you enter college or the workforce and maybe have a family. Developing good, consistent habits related to self-care now will serve you all your life!

Being prepared will help you feel less stressed during a job interview.

Interviewing Skills

Sooner or later, your job search will result in what you've been hoping for—or perhaps dreading: a phone call or e-mail requesting that you appear for an interview. When you get that call or e-mail, it means the employer is interested in and considering hiring you.

"Am I adaptive? Do I handle change well? Am I determined and can I commit myself to a project even when things appear difficult? How do I handle rigidity? Those are serious questions to ask yourself. People who are adaptive, people who know when and when not to be rigid—those are people who tend to excel in this field."—Trey Perry, VP of software architecture

The best way to avoid nerves and keep calm when you're interviewing is to be prepared. It's okay to feel scared, but keep it in perspective. It's likely that you'll receive many more rejections than acceptances in your professional life, as we all do. However, you only need one *yes* to start out. Think of the interviewing process as a learning experience. With the right attitude, you will learn from each one and get better with each subsequent interview. That should be your overarching goal. Consider these tips and tricks when interviewing, whether it be for a job, internship, college admission, or something else entirely:

- Practice interviewing with a friend or relative. Practicing will help calm your nerves and make you feel more prepared. Ask for specific feedback from your friends. Do you need to speak more loudly? Are you making enough eye contact? Are you actively listening when the other person is speaking?
- Learn as much as you can about the company, school, or organization, and be sure to understand the position for which you're applying. This will show the interviewer that you are motivated and interested in the organization.
- Speak up during the interview. Convey to the interviewer important points about yourself. Don't be afraid to ask questions. Try to remember the interviewers' names and call them by name.
- Arrive early and dress professionally and appropriately. (You can read more about proper dress in a following section.)
- Take some time to prepare answers to commonly asked questions. Be ready to describe your career or educational goals to the interviewer.[1]

Common questions you may be asked during a job interview include:

- Tell me about yourself.
- What are your greatest strengths?
- What are your weaknesses?
- Tell me something about yourself that's not on your résumé.
- What are your career goals?
- How do you handle failure? Are you willing to fail?
- How do you handle stress and pressure?
- What are you passionate about?
- Why do you want to work for us?

Bring a notebook and a pen to the interview. That way you can take some notes, and they'll give you something to do with your hands.

Common questions you may be asked during a college admissions interview include these:

- Tell me about yourself.
- Why are you interested in going to college?
- Why do you want to major in this subject?
- What are your academic strengths?
- What are your academic weaknesses? How have you addressed them?
- What will you contribute to this college/school/university?
- Where do you see yourself in ten years?
- How do you handle failure? Are you willing to fail?
- How do you handle stress and pressure?
- Whom do you most admire?
- What is your favorite book?
- What do you do for fun?
- Why are you interested in this college/school/university?

Jot down notes about your answers to these questions, but don't try to memorize the answers. You don't want to come off as too rehearsed during the interview. Remember to be as specific and detailed as possible when answering these questions. Your goal is to set yourself apart in some way from the other interviewees. Always accentuate the positive, even when you're asked about something you did not like, or about failure or stress. Most importantly, though, be yourself.

Active listening is the process of fully concentrating on what is being said, understanding it, and providing nonverbal cues and responses to the person talking.[2] It's the opposite of being distracted and thinking about something else when someone is talking. Active listening takes practice. You might find that your mind wanders and you need to bring your attention back to the person talking (and this could happen multiple times during one conversation). Practice this technique in regular conversations with friends and relatives. In addition to giving a better interview, it can cut down on nerves and make you more popular with friends and family, as everyone wants to feel that they are really being heard. For more on active listening, check out www.mindtools.com/CommSkll/ActiveListening.htm.

You should also be ready to ask questions of your interviewer. In a practical sense, there should be some questions you have that you can't find the answer to on the website or in the literature. Also, asking questions shows that you are interested and have done your homework. Avoid asking questions about salary, scholarships, or special benefits at this stage, and don't ask about anything negative you've heard about the company or school. Keep the questions positive and related to the position to which you're applying. Some example questions to potential employers include:

- What is a typical career path for a person in this position?
- How would you describe the ideal candidate for this position?
- How is the department organized?
- What kind of responsibilities come with this job? (Don't ask this if it has already been addressed in the job description or discussion.)
- What can I do as a follow-up?
- When do you expect to reach a decision?

See "Make the Most of School Visits" in chapter 3 for some good examples of questions to ask the college admissions office. The important thing is to write your own questions related to information you really want to know, and be sure your question isn't already answered on the website, in the job description, or in the literature. This will show genuine interest.

BLENDING IT AND BUSINESS
FOR A CAREER IN IT MANAGEMENT

Cary Chandler has been in love with computers and programming since about 1980, when he first learned to program on a Commodore VIC-20. But he also loves the business side of IT, and that led him to a degree in management information systems (MIS), which allows him to understand his clients' needs (and the needs of his own company) in a way that many traditional programmers can't.

Cary Chandler. *Courtesy of Cary Chandler.*

He has a lot to say about what it takes to succeed in the world of IT, how you can know if it's right for you, the difference between the hardware and software side of the industry, as well as tougher questions such as what it's like to look around a technical conference or workplace and not see anyone else like you there.

What is your current title and where do you work?

My current title is chief operations officer at Imavex, which is a web development and digital marketing firm in Fishers, Indiana.

What are your main job duties at Imavex?

My responsibility is the production of all web-related projects. So that's everything from when the project starts all the way through the finished product. I'm also responsible for client support and internal IT operations.

What's a brief recap of some other IT jobs that you've had?

Before my job at Imavex, I was the director of information systems at Riverview Hospital in Noblesville, Indiana. I was also the chief information officer at Riverview for at least nine months there on an interim role.

Before that, I was the director of application development at Allied Solutions in Carmel. I was in that position for nine years.

And before that, I was a senior consultant at a technology consulting firm called Whittman-Hart that became known as marchFIRST. This is during the real advent of the internet, particularly in business. The company really focused on a lot of technical consulting for companies, but got more into building websites: large websites and different projects.

Did you know early on, say, in high school or around then, that information technology is what you wanted to do?

I was lucky enough to find what I wanted to do at age twelve. So I actually started programming at age twelve and just dealing with the BASIC language on an old Commodore VIC-20 system, just building different games on the computer and using magazines to kind of supplement my code and learn different techniques.

When I went into high school, I was looking for a high school that at least had computers. I grew up in Chicago, so I was lucky enough that my parents could send me to a private school that was on the outskirts of the south side of Chicago, and they actually had Apple computers at the time. It was just an older Apple computer and they were teaching BASIC programming classes and Pascal. So I was able to get exposed to computers in high school.

I knew that that's what I wanted to do more than anything else in high school. So when I went into college, I was definitely looking for computer science programs and enrolled in computer science at Ball State.

I ended up coming out with a degree in MIS. I just found the business side appealed to me more, but I enjoyed the programming courses, so it was a good fit for me.

Computer science is one of those fields that you can just kind of branch out into a lot of different areas of science, business, and even more now, but I seem to understand the business side of it more than the actual scientific subjects.

Does the MIS degree really appeal to people who have sort of one foot in information technology and the other in a business mind-set?

Yes. It is a really good hybrid because you have to take the computer science courses, but you also take a lot of statistics and different business courses. We had to take basic accounting and cost accounting.

So all the different business courses I think made me a stronger candidate when I came out of school, and it helped me to understand what businesses wanted to do with technology, so I think it's a really good hybrid.

It still exists today. Some choose to go into computer science, but some actually choose to go into information systems.

Beyond the MIS degree from Ball State, you have a master's?

I started in the information and communication sciences master's program at Ball State. I did not complete that; I'm nine hours shy.

I had the opportunity to go work for Arthur Anderson in Chicago and I just took it. I thought I would be able to come back and finish my degree at Ball State, but it took a certain amount of time that my credits had expired, so I didn't get the opportunity to go back and finish that.

What sort of informal, not necessarily degree programs but certification programs do you think are important for someone in your field?

It's interesting because it's changed so much now, and I definitely have new staff that comes in and we have to get them some additional training.

On the technical side, I don't think we push the certifications as much just because the technology has a tendency to outgrow the certification. And back in the day, Microsoft certifications in Visual Basic or something like that were a really big thing, but it only lasts so long.

So we just kind of push more continued education and make sure employees can always go out and look for different online programs that they can get into, get a deeper knowledge of the technology, and we mentor them on trying to understand how to get additional information, how to learn more about technology, the different trade magazines that you might need to pay attention to, the different podcasts, and show them how to learn more about technology as opposed to certifications.

So instead of just, "Hey, this particular badge is important," it's more like whatever you're into, just keeping learning?

Yes. Get a deeper knowledge. If someone has a certification, we certainly view that with value and we'll compensate it, but I think what I've seen is because there's some of the certifications that people are working long and hard to get, they outgrew them and they did not become as useful anymore.

It's more important for a young person to actually learn how to learn additional things about the technology and where to go to learn more about a specific thing.

How does one go about learning more about JavaScript, for example? Well, there's online training, but there are additional online forums that you should get involved with too. Maybe working on certain open-source projects; they kind of build your core knowledge.

Doing those things is going to make them a stronger person in their field.

This might be a dumb question, but is it safe to say that if you are going into information technology, your education will never end?

Yes, 100 percent. I think you're always learning, and one of the things that I do quite a bit is listen to podcasts on different technologies just because I want to learn about them.

I subscribed to a lot of different magazines that I can read, but now most of it is online. I like to aggregate a lot of different opinions from people, so that I can read through them to see what technologies are the ones that are going to emerge.

It's a lot tougher now because new technologies don't last as long as they did back in the '90s. If I learned a new technology in the '90s, I could maybe have a year and a half to two years of core knowledge before people were able to catch up; well, now it's maybe six months.

I know there's no typical day, but what might be a typical day, a typical schedule for you?

Typical schedule is usually e-mail in the morning, to try and maybe set your day and see if there's any surprises overnight. In my area, you always have to look at operations to see if something happened overnight that was unexpected or is there something that we need to address from a client? And that's probably what I spend maybe the first hour of the day or two hours looking into.

Then I do project work, which is making sure that my team has everything they need to do their projects.

And I'm also working on projects too. I believe in the "working manager," where you're a manager, but you're also still working on a project. Even at Imavex, our CEO does this.

That's always just been what has happened or what I've seen in the IT field; the managers still work quite a bit.

Typically, I'll have meetings; sometimes you're meeting with vendors, sometimes you have internal meetings that require my attention, sometimes I have internal sales meetings where they want to bring me into a meeting to discuss a potential opportunity that we might have, and just kind of pick my brain on how we might approach it or what technology would work best for our client.

As you said before, there's no typical day.

Are there any ways you've been surprised in your job? Anything that you didn't expect?

I never anticipated the speed of change. That is something that's tough to adjust to because when you get this core knowledge of something, it changes.

The thought is, "Okay, I'll learn this particular language and then that's the language I'll work in for the rest of my life." I learned very early that that's not the case, that you have to continue to learn quite a bit.

So the speed of change was something that's unexpected. It gets uncomfortable at times, particularly when you're on the bottom part of it, and you have to learn a lot, but that was certainly something that I didn't expect.

I think that's maybe one of the issues that I have with new staff is that they get out of school and they're working, but they don't realize that you still have to extend it beyond the workday and in the evenings you need to do certain things to gain more additional knowledge.

So at work, we need you to work, but in your off hours, at night, we still need you to learn and build your own skill and take ownership of your own level of experience in technology. So those are definitely surprises.

Tell me about being a manager.

Becoming a manager means that maybe you're not going to be the best technical person anymore, and it means that you have to make yourself a little bit more vulnerable to those around you who are stronger on the technology side because they stayed in it; but it does require some to get out of the technology side but have an understanding of what the makeup is of technology and the people who are in there, and how they liked to be there, to actually do that role of leading them.

That's something that I've accepted. I think I do a really good job of doing that. The feedback that I get from my staff is they like being managed by me because I understand exactly who they are and what they like to do. I don't micromanage them. I don't try to tell them exactly how to do something. They want to be listened to and they want projects that kind of stoke their passion.

So because I understand that, it makes me a better leader to other technical people.

Give me the things you like best and like least about your industry.

I'll start with the good: The technology, and that would make sense because I've been in the field for so long that you have to love it.

I still love the technology. When I hear about a new technology, I can start reading about it or even get my hands on it, it's like, "Oh wow, that's great."

I love the thrill of learning something that's entirely new: a new concept and technology that could be prominent, before it's prominent.

So I still love the technology; that is something that I'll always love no matter what I do in my career.

The creativity: I love the creativity side of it. That's something that has picked up as I've been in the field; I've definitely embraced more the creative side of it and what can be created. So that's something that still gives me a lot of passion and energy every day.

The people: I really enjoy working with technical people, particularly on the software side, more so than a hardware side. I skew more on the software side than the hardware side, but I love the people that work in technology. I think they are some of the most interesting people in the world. You find that there're so many really entertaining and interesting facts about them.

They come from all different walks of life. Some come from families that are very wealthy, and some come from families that didn't have anything at all. But because the field itself has the tendency to skew more liberal it's very open and very accepting, and I think I found that too. I've embraced that and I found that to be very comfortable.

At the time when I first started going to conferences, maybe I was the only person of color there, but that's since changed. The field has gotten much more diverse now. It still has a ways to go, but even though I was maybe the only person of color there, I've never felt like I was different because there was this common bond over the appreciation of technology.

So that's always been good, and so those were obviously the things that I liked. I still enjoy that most about technology.

In that sense, you feel like it's a true meritocracy?

Yes, and you were never uncomfortable and you would look around and be like wow, I'm the only person of color here among this few thousand, but it was just never an issue. You can come together, you can collaborate, you can talk about code, and there was just always a very open environment and free thinking.

On the negative side, I would say that this industry does require a lot of time and you have to really balance it quite a bit.

Sometimes, the positive side of it is also a negative side of it. How things change, that can sometimes add a lot of stress. For some people, that's one of the things that they like the most. I wouldn't say it's something that I really hate, but it's challenging.

The time that's needed to be in the technology field, the time that it takes both throughout the day and at the end of the day is very challenging.

If it were something you didn't love, it might be even more challenging to stay in it.

Yes, and I've seen that happen with people, particularly in the '90s, probably the late '90s, when there are a lot of people that were going into a field because there were a lot of jobs, particularly as companies were embracing the internet, you can tell the ones who were in the field that really didn't enjoy it. They didn't have a passion for it; it was just a job.

So when the bust happened and people started losing their jobs, they're the ones that entered new fields. They basically just went in different areas, but the people who love the technology, even though they were losing their jobs, they were still finding another IT job. It was never a situation where you're just kind of moving into something completely different. You're going to find another IT job because that's what you did.

So that was definitely something I always remember. For me, the negatives aren't that big, and it's because I like IT. I've always liked it, so maybe you ignore some of the other areas that aren't as great.

When you sit back and think about your career, what's the dream job of someone in the IT field?

Probably research and development, because you're continually exposed to new technology, especially if you're lucky enough to work with someone that has a budget and there's no limit to it.

If you could work in research and development and you're not really dealing with production and the need to make a buck and you can just really sit there and play with the technology and get really deep into the knowledge of it, I think that's every technical person's dream.

And most of the people that I've worked with that really enjoy technology, they understand the business side of it, but deep down inside, they just kind of want to learn the technology as deeply as they can understand and see what they can do.

You knew early in life that you wanted to do this. But for students in middle school or high school who aren't sure what they want to do, what kind of questions should they ask themselves to determine if IT might be a good fit for them?

I think the first is to understand that one, technology is such an open area. See where you skew. Do you skew more on the software creative side or do you skew more on the hardware engineering side?

Do you want to tinker with different hardware and try to see how to build the next great smartphone or something like that? Well then, there're areas for you that you can go into that will really stoke your interests and your passions and that you can build a career on.

But if you're still one that's more on the creative side, you like building software, crafting things, then the software side is still a very open area for you, and it'll continue to be an open area for you. So you can certainly go in that direction.

Don't think that you have to be pigeonholed into one specific route into technology that is a very broad field; you just have to find where you fit in, what interests you the most. So I think that will be the first thing.

The other thing to ask yourself is, will you accept the fact that being in the field, you're going to have to learn continuously over and over? Is that something that you embrace?

This is really good particularly if you're dealing with kids and trying to explain to them that you have to take the time to really learn. Don't shy away from learning, particularly nowadays, where when you want to find an answer, you can just Google it.

You want to learn the concepts and spend the time to understand how something works. Just don't look for an answer. If you're someone who wants to look and see how something works, I'll say yes, it's going to be a great field for you.

If you're someone who just wants to get an answer, you can probably survive in IT, but I don't think you're really going to embrace it.

What are some of the challenges that the IT field will face in the next five years?

Definitely the competition, and that's because it's more of a global economy now. You could be competing for your job with someone in India or elsewhere outside United States.

So the competition is something that is difficult to deal with, and particularly for a newer person who's trying to learn the technology; it's like you've got competition not just from those local to you, you have competition from abroad. So that definitely is a challenge.

It's also the competition among different companies. A lot of people can do the same things that we do, you don't have the secret sauce, and trying to differentiate ourselves in what we do to a potential client? That's a lot more difficult today than it was probably twenty years ago.

When you're hiring someone for an entry-level job, who doesn't have to have a lot of experience, what do you look for in a candidate for a new job? What traits or what sort of knowledge or what street smarts do you look for?

That's a good question, because there are a lot of different things. One, I look to see: Is the person interesting? I think not just for myself, but for other developers that work on our staff, because they're all interesting, will they find this individual interesting and want to work with them? Because that just gives us a nice, cohesive team. So I look to see how interesting that person is.

I also really focus on this individual's strengths. Will their strengths actually help balance our team? Maybe they're strong in a certain area and our team is missing that. Maybe it's a user-interface guy and maybe they're strong on the front end, and our team is really not strong on the front end; if they're strong in that area and they can add value to our team, then I would certainly look to bring them in for that reason too.

I also look to see how well they learn. Do they embrace learning? How they spend their time outside of technology. Are they just so ingrained in technology, they're not thinking about anything else? I would rather that they be involved in different things as well, not just do technology by themselves.

For me a lot of times because of what we do, I look to see how creative they are. Are they someone that can take a blank slate and create something? That's important in the business that we're in today.

I do obviously look at the grades because that'll tell you how well they learn, but I also look to see if they [are] involved in different groups, to see how well they can work with others.

You talked about demographics at a conference; what words of encouragement do you have for women in technology, people of color, and people who might not be traditionally thought of as information technologists? What do you say to them?

I will certainly say that, from my own background, don't be afraid to try it and don't look around, like if you're in a classroom and you're the only female in there or you're the only person of color, don't allow that to distract you from the purpose, and understand that most technology people that at least I've encountered are pretty open-minded.

As long as you share that common bond or the common interest in something—maybe it's programming, maybe it's hardware—then you should pursue it and to try to learn more about them as you'll learn more about yourself as well.

Just don't allow what you see to scare you away from the field. Sometimes, I think people will get in the class and realize something like, "Wow, I'm the only female in the class," and that might scare them away, and it shouldn't. If you have that passion in technology, you should go for it and let nothing stop you.

Again, it's a very open field. I think it will continue to get more diverse. In my classes, I don't think there was a female in any of my classes at Ball State, but one of our new hires is a woman with a computer science degree from Ball State. She brings to our team a different perspective. She's respected and she's looked upon as another developer. I don't think we see her in any way differently, but she definitely brings different perspectives, which makes our team strong.

What would you say to parents whose kids are interested in IT?

Parents, if you have a child that is interested in technology, support that. They may get called a nerd or something like that, because my brother certainly did, and I was in athletics in high school too, so when I wasn't at practice, I was in the computer lab. It was like two different worlds

Having supportive parents stay behind you and do those things for you meant a lot. I'm always very appreciative of them and I try to do the same thing for our kids today. No matter what it is, we stand behind them and help them try to learn more about it.

DRESSING APPROPRIATELY

It's important to determine what is actually appropriate in the setting of the interview. What is appropriate in a corporate setting might be different from what you'd expect at a small liberal arts college or at a large hospital setting. For example, most college admissions offices suggest business casual attire, but depending on the job interview, you may want to step it up from there. Again, it's important to do your homework and come prepared. In addition to reading up on the organization's guidelines, it never hurts to take a look around the website if you can to see what other people are wearing to work or to interviews. Regardless of the setting, make sure your clothes are not wrinkled, untidy, or stained. Avoid flashy clothing of any kind.

The term *business casual* means less formal than business attire (like a suit), but a step up from jeans, a T-shirt, and sneakers.

- *For men:* You can't go wrong with khaki pants, a polo or button-up shirt, and brown or black shoes.
- *For women:* Wear nice slacks, a shirt or blouse that isn't too revealing, and nice flats or shoes with a heel that's not too high.

Do the proper research to find out exactly how you should dress for your interview.

Follow-Up Communication

Be sure to follow up, whether via e-mail or regular mail, with a thank-you note to the interviewer. This is appropriate whether you're interviewing for a job or an internship, or interviewing with a college. A handwritten thank-you note, posted in the mail, is best. In addition to showing consideration, it will trigger the interviewer's memory about you and it shows that you have genuine interest in the position, company, or school. Be sure to follow the business letter format and highlight the key points of your interview and experience at the company or university. Be prompt with your thank-you note! Put it in the mail the day after your interview or send that e-mail the same day.

What Employers Expect

Regardless of the job, profession, or field, there are universal characteristics that all employers—and schools, for that matter—look for in candidates. At this early stage in your professional life, you have an opportunity to recognize which of these foundational characteristics are your strengths (and therefore highlight them in an interview) and which are weaknesses (and therefore continue to work on them and build them up).

> Always aim to make your boss's job easier, not harder. Keeping this simple concept in mind can take you a very long way in the business world. By the same token, being able to convince an employer that you love to learn new things is one of the best ways to turn yourself into a candidate they won't be able to pass up.

Consider these characteristics:

- Positive attitude
- Dependability
- Desire to continue to learn
- Initiative
- Effective communication

- Cooperation
- Organization

This is not an exhaustive list, and other desirable characteristics include things like sensitivity to others, honesty, good judgment, loyalty, responsibility, and punctuality. Specific to IT, you can add self-motivation, patience, perseverance, attention to detail, and self-control. Consider these important characteristics when you answer the common questions that employers ask. It pays to work these traits into the answers—of course, being honest and realistic about yourself.

Beware the social media trap! Prospective employers and colleges will check your social media sites, so make sure there is nothing too personal, explicit, or inappropriate out there. When you communicate to the world on social media, don't use profanity—and be sure to use proper grammar. Think about the version of yourself you are portraying online. Is it favorable, or at least neutral, to potential employers? Rest assured: They will look.

Personal contacts can make the difference! Don't be afraid to contact other professionals you know. Personal connections can be a great way to find jobs and internship opportunities. Your high school teachers, your coaches and mentors, and your friends' parents are all examples of people who very well may know about jobs or opportunities that would suit you. Start asking several months before you hope to start a job or internship, because it will take some time to do research and arrange interviews. You can also use social media in your search. LinkedIn (www.linkedin.com), for example, includes lots of searchable information on local companies. Follow and interact with people on social media to get their attention. Just remember to act professionally and communicate with proper grammar, just as you would in person.

No matter which field you choose in IT, demand is high for this career!

Summary

Well, you made it to the end of this book! Hopefully, you have learned enough about the IT field to start along your journey, or to continue along your path. If you've reached the end and you feel like computers are your passion, that's great news. If you've figured out that it isn't the right field for you, that's good information to learn, too. For many of us, figuring out what we *don't* want to do and what we *don't* like is an important step in finding the right career.

> "Good IT people will lack ego, listen well, enjoy challenges, be comfortable not immediately knowing answers and also owning mistakes. Anyone uncomfortable with these things will have a difficult time in most any field, not just IT."—Scott Dafforn, senior full-stack developer

There is a lot of good news about the IT field, and it's a very smart career choice for anyone with a passion for computers. It's a great career for people who get energy from solving problems. Job demand is very strong. Whether you decide to be a hard-core programmer or want to focus on web development, having a plan and an idea about your future can help guide your decisions. After reading this book, you should be well on your way to having a plan for your future. Good luck to you as you move ahead!

Notes

Chapter 1

1. Bureau of Labor Statistics, "Computer Support Specialists: What Computer Support Specialists Do," https://www.bls.gov/ooh/computer-and-information-technology/computer-support-specialists.htm#tab-2.

2. Bureau of Labor Statistics, "Computer Support Specialists: Pay," https://www.bls.gov/ooh/computer-and-information-technology/computer-support-specialists.htm#tab-5.

3. Bureau of Labor Statistics, "Computer Programmers: Pay," https://www.bls.gov/ooh/computer-and-information-technology/computer-programmers.htm#tab-5.

4. Bureau of Labor Statistics, "Web Developers: Job Outlook," https://www.bls.gov/ooh/computer-and-information-technology/web-developers.htm#tab-6.

5. Bureau of Labor Statistics, "Web Developers: Pay," https://www.bls.gov/ooh/computer-and-information-technology/web-developers.htm#tab-5.

6. Bureau of Labor Statistics, "Web Developers: How to Become a Web Developer," https://www.bls.gov/ooh/computer-and-information-technology/web-developers.htm#tab-4.

7. Bureau of Labor Statistics, "Computer Systems Analysts: What Computer Systems Analysts Do," https://www.bls.gov/ooh/computer-and-information-technology/computer-systems-analysts.htm#tab-2.

8. Bureau of Labor Statistics, "Computer Systems Analysts: Pay," https://www.bls.gov/ooh/computer-and-information-technology/computer-systems-analysts.htm#tab-5.

9. Ibid.

10. Bureau of Labor Statistics, "Computer Systems Analysts: How to Become a Computer Systems Analyst," https://www.bls.gov/ooh/computer-and-information-technology/computer-systems-analysts.htm#tab-4.

11. Bureau of Labor Statistics, "Computer Network Architects: What Computer Network Architects Do," https://www.bls.gov/ooh/computer-and-information-technology/computer-network-architects.htm#tab-2.

12. Bureau of Labor Statistics, "Computer Network Architects: Job Outlook," https://www.bls.gov/ooh/computer-and-information-technology/computer-network-architects.htm#tab-6.

13. Bureau of Labor Statistics, "Information Security Analysts: What Information Security Analysts Do," https://www.bls.gov/ooh/computer-and-information-technology/information-security-analysts.htm#tab-2.

14. Bureau of Labor Statistics, "Information Security Analysts: Pay," https://www.bls.gov/ooh/computer-and-information-technology/information-security-analysts.htm#tab-5.

15. Bureau of Labor Statistics, "Information Security Analysts: How to Become an Information Security Analyst," https://www.bls.gov/ooh/computer-and-information-technology/information-security-analysts.htm#tab-4.

Chapter 2

1. Gene Linetsky, "How to Become a Programmer," WikiHow, https://www.wikihow.com/Become-a-Programmer.

2. "Web Programming," *Technopedia*, https://www.techopedia.com/definition/23898/web-programming.

3. Linetsky, "How to Become a Programmer."

4. "Web Developer," *Wikipedia*, https://en.wikipedia.org/wiki/Web_developer.

5. Cisco, "Certifications," https://www.cisco.com/c/en/us/training-events/training-certifications/certifications.html.

6. https://www.bls.gov/ooh/computer-and-information-technology/information-security-analysts.htm

7. https://www.bls.gov/ooh/computer-and-information-technology/information-security-analysts.htm#tab-4

8. Lou Adler, "New Survey Reveals 85% of All Jobs Are Filled via Networking," LinkedIn, February 29, 2016, https://www.linkedin.com/pulse/new-survey-reveals-85-all-jobs-filled-via-networking-lou-adler/.

Chapter 3

1. Gap Year Association, "Gap Year Data & Benefits," https://www.gapyearassociation.org/data-benefits.php.

2. Peter Van Buskirk, "Finding a Good College Fit," *U.S. News & World Report*, June 13, 2011, https://www.usnews.com/education/blogs/the-college-admissions-insider/2011/06/13/finding-a-good-college-fit.

3. National Center for Education Statistics, "Fast Facts: Graduation Rates," https://nces.ed.gov/fastfacts/display.asp?id=40.

4. Department of Education, National Center for Education Statistics, "Table 502.30: Median Annual Earnings of Full-Time Year-Round Workers 25 to 34 Years Old and Full-Time Year-Round Workers as a Percentage of the Labor Force, by Sex, Race/Ethnicity, and Educational Attainment: Selected Years, 1995 through 2013," *Digest for Education Statistics*, https://nces.ed.gov/programs/digest/d14/tables/dt14_502.30.asp.

5. Anthony P. Carnevale, "The Economic Value of College Majors Executive Summary 2015," Georgetown University Center on Education and the Workforce, McCourt School of Public Policy (2015): 1–44.

6. College Board, "Understanding College Costs," https://bigfuture.college|board.org/pay-for-college/college-costs/understanding-college-costs.

7. Federal Student Aid, US Department of Education, "FAFSA Changes for 2017–2018," https://studentaid.ed.gov/sa/fafsa/filling-out.

Chapter 4

1. Justin Ross Muchnick, *Teens' Guide to College & Career Planning*, 12th ed. (Lawrenceville, NJ: Peterson's, 2015), 179–80.

2. Mind Tools, "Active Listening: Hear What People Are Really Saying," http://www.mindtools.com/CommSkll/ActiveListening.htm.

Glossary

accreditation: The act of officially recognizing an organizational body, person, or educational facility as having a particular status or being qualified to perform a particular activity. For example, schools and colleges are accredited. *See also* **certification**.

ACT: One of the standardized college entrance tests that anyone wanting to enter undergraduate studies in the United States should take. It measures knowledge and skills in mathematics, English, reading, and science reasoning as they apply to college readiness. There are four multiple-choice sections and an optional writing test. The total score of the ACT is 36. *See also* **SAT**.

application: A computer program written in a programming language that serves a coordinated purpose for its users, such as a word processing application. Other examples of applications include spreadsheet apps like Excel, web browsers that enable you to view web pages on the internet, and graphics editors like Photoshop. *See also* **web app** and **code**.

associate's degree: A degree awarded by a community or junior college that typically requires two years of study.

bachelor's degree: An undergraduate degree awarded by a college or university that is typically a four-year course of study when pursued full-time. However, this can vary by degree earned and by the university awarding the degree.

back end: In context of IT, the back end of a computer system typically refers to the portion that stores or manipulates data. It is not usually visible or accessible to the users. Often also called the server side, this is the physical infrastructure or hardware. Back-end developers might write code for the server, the database, the operating system, or the actual software. *See also* **front end**.

certification: The action or process of confirming that an individual has acquired certain skills or knowledge, usually provided by some third-party review, assessment, or educational body. Individuals, not organizations, are certified. *See also* **accreditation**.

cloud computing: In a cloud computing system, the computer resources (such as storage and computing power) are available on demand at a centralized data center (called the cloud), not on the user's computer. Often, the internet serves as the cloud, but clouds can also be run from a centralized data center in a single organization (called an enterprise cloud) or there can be third-party clouds used by multiple organizations (public clouds). There can also be a combination of these two types, called hybrid clouds. Benefits of cloud computing include economies of scale, reduced IT infrastructure costs, better response to changing demands, and quicker adaptations to updates and changes.

code: A set of instructions and commands read by a computer. Also called a programming language, code comes in many varieties for different uses, including assembly, compiled, interpreted, and object-oriented languages. *See also* **programming language**.

cybersecurity: A set of techniques put in place to protect the safety and integrity of networks and other internet-connected systems from attacks. This includes securing their hardware, software, and data.

database: A collection of data in a computer that is organized into tables and schemas and can be accessed and reviewed to create useful reports. The data is presented in a model that represents an actual physical object that is familiar to users, such as a folder. Commercially successful databases include Microsoft Access, SQL Server, and Oracle DB.

DevOps: Software development methods that endeavor to shorten the time between making a change to a computer system and the incorporation of that change into the system, all the while focusing on accuracy and quality. This philosophy emphasizes collaboration and communication between software developers (*Dev*) and other IT professionals (*Ops*). The goal is to deliver new features and updates, as well as fixes, quickly and often. DevOps uses the practices of continuous integration and continuous delivery, among other approaches, to achieve this mode of working. Very similar to the *Agile* software development movement.

doctoral degree: The highest level of degree awarded by colleges and universities. This degree qualifies the holder to teach at the university level and requires (usually published) research in the field. Earning a doctoral degree typically requires an additional three to five years of study after earning a bachelor's degree. Anyone with a doctoral degree—not just medical doctors—can be addressed as "Doctor."

front end: In context of IT, the front end of a computer system usually refers to the interface layer that the user interacts with, also often called the client side or the presentation layer. Front-end development is typically concerned with how information is presented to the users. *See also* **back end**.

full-stack developer: An IT engineer who can work with and manage all databases, servers, systems engineering components, and clients. Depending on the project, customers may need a mobile *stack*, a web *stack*, or a native application *stack*.

gap year: A year between high school and college (or sometimes between college and postgraduate studies) during which the student is not in school but is instead involved in other pursuits, typically volunteer programs such as the Peace Corps, in travel experiences, or in work and teaching experiences.

grants: Money to pay for postsecondary education that is typically awarded to students who have financial need, but can also be used in the areas of athletics, academics, demographics, veteran support, and special talents. Grants do not have to be paid back.

hardware: The physical parts of the computer system, such as the actual machines, cards, wires, keyboards, and other parts, both external and internal. If you can hold it in your hand, it's part of the hardware system. *See also* **software** *and* **peripherals**.

information security analyst: An IT professional who plans and carries out security measures to protect an organization's computer networks and systems.

master's degree: A postgraduate degree awarded by a college or university that requires at least one additional year of study after obtaining a bachelor's degree. The degree holder shows mastery of a specific field.

network: A group of connected computers that exchange data with each other. They are connected via some kind of telecommunications network made up of wires or cables, or via wireless media. The internet is an example of a computer network.

network engineer: An IT professional who focuses on computer network and system administration. Because administrators work with computer hardware and equipment, a degree in computer engineering or electrical engineering is often desirable in this field.

open source: A type of software in which the original source code is released under a license whereby the copyright holder grants users the rights to study, change, and distribute the software to anyone and for any purpose. Open-source software may be developed in a collaborative public manner. Benefits of using open-source software include lower software and hardware costs and solid support and maintenance from the open-source community.

operating system (OS): The system software that controls the computer's hardware and software systems and defines how they interact. Examples of common operating systems include MacOS, Windows, Linux, and DOS. Software applications that run on a specific computer are often OS dependent, in that they are written specifically for a certain OS and can't be run on any others. *See also* **web app**.

peripherals: Specific types of computer hardware input or output devices that give computers additional functionality. Strictly speaking, peripherals are not required for the computer to run. Examples include thumb drives, sound cards, speakers, printers, joysticks, mice, and keyboards. Peripherals cannot operate by themselves; they need a computer in order to function. *See also* **hardware**.

personal statement: A written description of your accomplishments, outlook, interests, goals, and personality that is an important part of your college application. The personal statement should set you apart from other applicants. The required length depends on the institution, but they generally range from one to two pages, or five hundred to one thousand words.

postsecondary degree: An educational degree above and beyond a high school education. This is a general description that includes trade certificates and certifications; associate's, bachelor's, and master's degrees; and beyond.

programmer: A general term for a person (or machine) who writes code and creates and tests computer programs. Programmers usually specialize in one or a few programming languages. Areas of expertise include software development, database development, hardware programming, and web development.

programming language: A formal language that communicates to a computer through its applications and programs. These programs are created from instructions and commands written in the programming language by developers. Examples of widely used programming languages include C#, Java, Python, and Visual Basic. *See also* **code**.

SAT: One of the standardized tests in the United States that anyone applying to undergraduate studies should take. It measures verbal and mathematical reasoning abilities as they relate to predicting successful performance in college. It is intended to complement a student's GPA and school record in assessing readiness for college. The total score of the SAT is 1600. *See also* **ACT**.

scholarships: Merit-based aid used to pay for postsecondary education that does not have to be paid back. Scholarships are typically awarded based on academic excellence or some other special talent, such as music or art.

software: The programs written in a programming language that run on the computer and operate its various functions. These are the instructions that tell the computer how to work and what to do, and are usually platform/OS dependent. *See also* **code**.

support: Computer support professionals provide advice and help to users having issues with their computer software and hardware. Their job is to troubleshoot, identify, and fix problems with single computers or networks under their purview.

web app: An application that runs in a web browser. A common example is a webmail application like Gmail, which stores your account data (your e-mail) in the Google cloud. You can access a web app from any computer connected to the internet using a standard browser. Web apps are typically platform/OS independent since the website serves as the user interface.

web development: A broad term that refers to the varied tasks involved in creating a website or web app, which will be hosted on the internet or on a local intranet. Web development includes designing the interface and the website; creating, programming, testing, and formatting the web content; client-side/server-side scripting for handling user interactions; managing and configuring network security; and more.

Further Resources

Are you looking for more information about the professions in information technology, or do you want to learn more about a particular area of IT? Do you want to know more about the college application process or need some help finding the right educational fit for you? Do you want a quick way to search for a good college or school? Try these resources as a starting point on your journey toward finding a fulfilling career as an IT specialist!

Books

Althoff, Cory. *The Self-Taught Programmer: The Definitive Guide to Programming Professionally*. San Francisco: Triangle Connection Press, 2017.

Bolles, Richard N. *What Color Is Your Parachute? A Practical Manual for Job-Hunters and Career-Changers*. Revised edition. Berkeley, CA: Ten Speed Press, 2018.

Fiske, Edward. *Fiske Guide to Colleges*. Naperville, IL: Sourcebooks, 2018.

Muchnick, Justin Ross. *Teens' Guide to College & Career Planning*, 12th ed. Lawrenceville, NJ: Peterson's, 2015.

Princeton Review. *The Best 382 Colleges, 2018 Edition: Everything You Need to Make the Right College Choice*. New York: Princeton Review, 2018.

Websites

American Gap Year Association
www.gapyearassociation.org
The American Gap Year Association's mission is "making transformative gap years an accessible option for all high school graduates." A gap year is a year taken between high school and college to travel, teach, work, volunteer, gener-

ally mature, and otherwise experience the world. The website has lots of advice and resources for anyone considering taking a gap year.

The Balance
www.thebalance.com
This site is all about managing money and finances, but also has a large section called Your Career, which provides advice for writing résumés and cover letters, interviewing, and more. Search the site for teens and you can find teen-specific advice and tips.

Codecademy
www.codecademy.com
This website is an effective and easy way to learn to code. It includes short modules on HTML, CSS, and website development, after which you can move on to other programming languages. The courses are easy to follow and the site awards badges when you finish each one, which can be a nice motivator to keep learning.

Codewars
www.codewars.com
This site is run by a community of developers who attempt to improve their development skills through challenges set by fellow members. It's similar to a coding dojo, where developers train with each other and help each other get better through practice. This is a great site once you have a little experience under your belt with beginner sites.

The College Entrance Examination Board
www.collegeboard.org
The College Entrance Examination Board tracks and summarizes financial data from colleges and universities all over the United States. This great, well-organized site can be your one-stop shop for all things college research. It contains lots of advice and information about taking and doing well on the SAT and ACT, many articles on college planning, a robust college search feature, a scholarship search feature, and a major and career search area. You can type your career of interest (for example, computer systems analysts) into the search box and get back a full page that describes the career; gives advice on how to

prepare, where to get experience, and how to pay for it; describes what characteristics you should have to excel in this career; lists helpful classes to take while in high school; and provides lots of links for more information.

College Grad Career Profiles
www.collegegrad.com/careers

Although this site is primarily geared toward college graduates, the career profiles area, indicated above, has a list of links to nearly every career you could ever think of. A single click takes you to a very detailed, helpful section that describes the job in detail, explains the educational requirements, includes links to good colleges that offer this career, includes links to actual open jobs and internships, describes the licensing requirements (if any), lists salaries, and much more.

GoCollege
www.gocollege.com

This site, which calls itself the number one college-bound website on the internet, includes lots of good tips and information about getting money and scholarships for college and getting the most out of your college education. The site has a good section on how scholarships in general work.

Go Overseas
www.gooverseas.com

This site, which claims to be your guide to more than sixteen thousand study and teach abroad programs that will change how you see the world, also includes information about high school abroad programs and gap year opportunities, as well as community reviews and information about finding programs specific to subject areas like cyber security, information technology, and programming.

Khan Academy
www.khanacademy.org

The Khan Academy website is an impressive collection of articles, courses, and videos about many educational topics in math, science, and the humanities. You can search any topic or subject (by subject matter and grade), and read lessons, take courses, and watch videos to learn all about it. The site includes test prep information for the SAT, ACT, AP, GMAT, and other standardized tests.

There is also a College Admissions tab with lots of good articles and information, provided in the approachable Khan style.

Krebs on Security
www.krebsonsecurity.com
Brian Krebs worked as a reporter for the *Washington Post* from 1995 to 2009, authoring more than thirteen hundred blog posts for the *Security Fix* blog. This site is his personal blog, which covers in depth security news and investigations, with a focus on cybercrime and other major data breaches and hacks.

Live Career
www.livecareer.com
This site has an impressive number of resources directed toward teens for writing résumés and cover letters, as well as interviewing.

Mapping Your Future
www.mappingyourfuture.org
This site helps young people figure out what they want to do and maps out how to reach career goals. Includes helpful tips on résumé writing, job hunting, job interviewing, and more.

Modern Analyst
www.modernanalyst.com
This site, a community and resource portal for business analyst and systems analyst professionals, includes webinars, forums, job postings, and more.

Monster.com
www.monster.com
This is perhaps the most well-known and certainly one of the largest employment websites in the United States. You fill in a couple of search boxes and away you go. You can sort by job title, of course, as well as by company name, location, salary range, experience range, and much more. The site also includes information about career fairs, advice on résumés and interviewing, and more.

Network World
www.networkworld.com
This magazine-style website focuses on network news, trend analysis, and product testing. It also includes many of the industry's most important blogs. It's considered one of the most active and frequent publishers of network-related content on the internet.

Occupational Outlook Handbook
www.bls.gov/ooh
The US Bureau of Labor Statistics produces this website, which offers lots of relevant and updated information about various careers, including average salaries, how to work in the industry, job market outlook, typical work environments, and what workers do on the job. See www.bls.gov/emp for a full list of employment projections.

Peterson's College Prep
www.petersons.com
In addition to lots of information about preparing for the ACT and SAT and easily searchable information about scholarships nationwide, the Peterson's site includes a comprehensive search feature for universities and schools based on location, major, name, and more.

Princeton Review Career Quiz
www.princetonreview.com/quiz/career-quiz
This site includes a very good aptitude test geared toward high schoolers to help them determine their interests and find professions that complement those interests.

Smashing Magazine
www.smashingmagazine.com
A reliable, venerable resource for web designers and developers looking to be inspired, *Smashing Magazine* publishes great content almost every day. In addition to links to articles and books, the site includes information about upcoming conferences and workshops as well as job postings for web developers.

Study.com
www.study.com
Similar to Khan Academy, Study.com allows you to search any topic or subject and read lessons, take courses, and watch videos to learn all about it. The site includes many IT and programming-related topics that will give you a taste of subjects you might with to study later on.

TeenLife
www.teenlife.com
This site calls itself "the leading source for college preparation," and it includes lots of information about summer programs, gap year programs, community service, and more. Promoting the belief that spending time out "in the world" outside of the classroom can help students develop important life skills, this site contains lots of links to volunteer and summer programs.

U.S. News & World Report *College Rankings*
www.usnews.com/best-colleges
U.S. News & World Report provides almost fifty different types of numerical rankings and lists of colleges throughout the United States to help students with their college search. You can search colleges by best reviewed, best value for the money, best liberal arts schools, best schools for B students, and more.

W3Schools
www.w3schools.com
This well-organized, easy-to-navigate site contains tutorials on all topics programming related, including lots of examples. Topics include learn HTML, learn CSS, learn Bootstrap, learn JavaScript, learn C++, learn XML, and many, many more. This site is frequented by newbies and senior developers alike, due to its depth and breadth of topics.

Web Designer Wall
www.webdesignerwall.com
This blog by Nick La features creative design ideas and detailed, striking tutorials such as creating text effects and getting started with jQuery, to name just a few.

Bibliography

"Blockchain." *Wikipedia*. https://en.wikipedia.org/wiki/Blockchain.

Bureau of Labor Statistics, US Department of Labor. "Computer and Information Technology Occupations." https://www.bls.gov/ooh/computer -and-information-technology/home.htm.

Indeed. "IT Jobs." https://www.indeed.com/q-IT-jobs.html.

Malvik, Callie. "9 Programming Careers for Programming Connoisseurs." Rasmussen College. https://www.rasmussen.edu/degrees/technology/blog/ programming-careers-for-coding-connoisseurs/.

Robert Half International. "10 Highest Paying IT Certifications for Tech Pros." https://www.roberthalf.com/blog/salaries-and-skills/10-highest-paying-it-certifications-for-tech-pros.

Skillcrush. "Front End, Back End, Full Stack—What Does It All Mean?" https://skillcrush.com/2017/02/27/front-end-back-end-full-stack/.

Toptal. "Back End Web Developer Job Description Template." https://www. toptal.com/back-end/job-description.

About the Author

Erik Dafforn is a writer and technical consultant from Indianapolis, Indiana, where he helps organizations with search engine optimization and analytics issues. His hobbies include cooking, running, and traveling with his wife and three children.

EDITORIAL BOARD

Eric Evitts has been working with teens in the high school setting for twenty-three years. Most of his career has dealt with getting teens, especially at-risk students, to find and follow a career path of interest. He has developed curriculum for Frederick County Public Schools focusing on anti-bullying and career development. He is currently a counselor at South Hagerstown High School.

Danielle Irving-Johnson, MA, EdS, is currently the career services specialist at the American Counseling Association. She exercises her specialty in career counseling by providing career guidance, services, and resources designed to encourage and assist students and professionals in obtaining their educational, employment, and career goals while also promoting the importance of self-care, wellness, work-life balance, and burnout prevention. Danielle has also previously served as a mental health counselor and clinical intake assessor in community agency settings assisting diverse populations with various diagnoses.

Joyce Rhine Shull, BS, MS, is an active member of the Maryland Association of Community College's Career Affinity Group and the Maryland Career Development Association. She presently serves as an academic adviser in higher education, and teaches Professionalism in the Workplace as an adjunct professor. Her experience also includes two decades of management and career education of vocational courses and seminars for high school students.

Lisa Adams Somerlot is the president of the American College Counseling Association and also serves as director of counseling at the University of West Georgia. She has a PhD in counselor education from Auburn University and is a licensed professional counselor in Georgia and is a nationally approved clinical supervisor. She is certified in Myers-Briggs Type Indicator, Strong Interest Inventory, and StrengthsQuest administration.